Out and About in Alderney

Out and About in Alderney

by
Brian Bonnard

The Guernsey Press Company Ltd.

© Brian Bonnard

All rights reserved. No part of this publication may be reproduced, stored in a retrieval system, or transmitted in any form or by any means, electronic, mechanical, photocopying, recording or otherwise, without the prior permission of Brian Bonnard

First published 1995

Made and printed in Great Britain by
The Guernsey Press Co. Ltd, Guernsey, Channel Islands.

ISBN 0 902550 55 1

By the Same Author;
Flora of Alderney; a Checklist with Notes, 1988, with corrections;
and additions to 1994. Price £3.50
The Island of Dread in the Channel, 1991. Price £14.99
Alderney in Old Photographs, 1991. Out of print
Wrecked around Alderney, 1993. Out of print
Alderney at War, 1993. Price £14.99
Alderney in Old Photographs; a Second series, 1993. Price £7.99
Channel Island Plant Lore, 1993. Price £4.95

DEDICATION
To all who love Alderney

CONTENTS

	Page
Map of Alderney	Endpaper
Introduction	1
Walks in Alderney	6

1. The Town Area
Walk 1.	Starting from the Albert Gate	8

2. The South Coast
Walk 2.	The Giffoine to Little Street	32
Walk 3.	Little Street to La Hêche	46
Walk 4.	La Hêche to La Tchue	51
Walk 5.	La Tchue to the Nunnery	56

3. The West Coast
Walk 6.	The Giffoine to Platte Saline	67
Walk 7.	The Zig-Zag to Platte Saline	77

4. The North Coast
Walk 8.	Butes to Platte Saline and Harbour and return via Braye and York Hill	80
Walk 9.	Butes to Harbour and Arsenal and return via Newtown	90
Walk 10.	Whitegates to Fort Albert, Saye, Château à L'Etoc and return	98

5. The East Coast
Walk 11.	Château à L'Etoc to the Nunnery	103

6. Inland Walks
Walk 12.	The Pottery to La Bonne Terre Platte Saline and return	118
Walk 13.	Inchalla Hotel, Water Lanes to Newtown and return	125
Walk 14.	Inchalla Hotel, Valongis to Newtown and return by Les Rochers	128
Walk 15.	Val Fontaine, La Haize and Barrack Master's Lane	131

Alderney by Car	134

INTRODUCTION

Braye Harbour from Butes

Alderney is a paradise for visitors, both young and old.

It is quiet, safe, almost free from crime and largely unspoilt by unsightly development or the widespread use of the agricultural sprays and farming techniques now so commonly used on the mainland, often to the detriment of both landscape and wildlife.

Alderney has a unique atmosphere, aided by the charm of its cobbled streets in St Anne, usually simply known as "Town". Its varied and slightly old-fashioned shopfronts, its splendid church of St. Anne, sometimes referred to as the "Cathedral of the Channel Islands", its friendly people and the generally unhurried pace of life, are all reminiscent of a bygone era. It is ideal for a family holiday, for the walker, the naturalist, the retired or those just seeking to get away from the hustle and bustle of large hotels and busy resorts. At the same time it does not suffer from many of the noisy attractions or night life often found in those places.

Guide books to holiday places invariably contain a lot of information, about the present day local facilities and places of interest, and about the history and natural history of the area, which their authors think the visitor might like to know.

This book tries to put most of this sort of information in a form easily and quickly absorbed by our visitors as they go about the island, giving such information as is relevant to the places they pass on the way. Thus it hopes to enhance the pleasure of their walks and drives, without boring them with unnecessary detail.

You can find out what is going on during your stay, and about most of the clubs and societies and their meetings, which are often open to visitors, by buying the current issue of The Alderney Journal, a fortnightly publication available from many outlets in the island. You are already here so there is little point in giving information about how to get here and the hotel and guest house facilities, etc. but a number of useful leaflets can be obtained from the Tourist Office in Victoria Street or the Harbour Office.

Alderney is different from any of the other Channel Islands in many ways.

It is home to about 800 species of plants, 260 birds, 7 Dragonflies, many Butterflies and moths, 1 reptile, 10 small land mammals and a lot of Victorian and German fortifications. Some of the wildlife is unique to Alderney or at least rarely found elsewhere in the British Islands. Conversely many plants, birds, hundreds of butterflies, dragonflies and moths and several mammals, common in the UK, are totally absent.

Like Jersey, Guernsey and Sark, it has its own system of government, here with an elected President of the "States", (as the three larger island's parliaments are called) and 12 elected members. It is however very largely dependent on Guernsey, who collect the taxes and administer Alderney's school,

INTRODUCTION

Braye Harbour from Butes

Alderney is a paradise for visitors, both young and old.

It is quiet, safe, almost free from crime and largely unspoilt by unsightly development or the widespread use of the agricultural sprays and farming techniques now so commonly used on the mainland, often to the detriment of both landscape and wildlife.

Alderney has a unique atmosphere, aided by the charm of its cobbled streets in St Anne, usually simply known as "Town". Its varied and slightly old-fashioned shopfronts, its splendid church of St. Anne, sometimes referred to as the "Cathedral of the Channel Islands", its friendly people and the generally unhurried pace of life, are all reminiscent of a bygone era. It is ideal for a family holiday, for the walker, the naturalist, the retired or those just seeking to get away from the hustle and bustle of large hotels and busy resorts. At the same time it does not suffer from many of the noisy attractions or night life often found in those places.

Guide books to holiday places invariably contain a lot of information, about the present day local facilities and places of interest, and about the history and natural history of the area, which their authors think the visitor might like to know.

This book tries to put most of this sort of information in a form easily and quickly absorbed by our visitors as they go about the island, giving such information as is relevant to the places they pass on the way. Thus it hopes to enhance the pleasure of their walks and drives, without boring them with unnecessary detail.

You can find out what is going on during your stay, and about most of the clubs and societies and their meetings, which are often open to visitors, by buying the current issue of The Alderney Journal, a fortnightly publication available from many outlets in the island. You are already here so there is little point in giving information about how to get here and the hotel and guest house facilities, etc. but a number of useful leaflets can be obtained from the Tourist Office in Victoria Street or the Harbour Office.

Alderney is different from any of the other Channel Islands in many ways.

It is home to about 800 species of plants, 260 birds, 7 Dragonflies, many Butterflies and moths, 1 reptile, 10 small land mammals and a lot of Victorian and German fortifications. Some of the wildlife is unique to Alderney or at least rarely found elsewhere in the British Islands. Conversely many plants, birds, hundreds of butterflies, dragonflies and moths and several mammals, common in the UK, are totally absent.

Like Jersey, Guernsey and Sark, it has its own system of government, here with an elected President of the "States", (as the three larger island's parliaments are called) and 12 elected members. It is however very largely dependent on Guernsey, who collect the taxes and administer Alderney's school, hospital, the airport, part of the small Civil Service, Police and Customs officers pay and conditions, pensions, family allowances, sick pay, etc. from the proceeds. Alderney has little say in how its funds are used for these purposes.

The States can pass Laws known as Orders-in-Council (which are drawn up for Alderney by H.M. Procureur in Guernsey, in accordance with the Projets de Lois previously passed in the States). They then have to come back to Alderney for States to accept them as written, then be approved in Guernsey States before they are sent to the Privy Council by the Lt. Governor, to receive the Royal Assent. Local Ordinances are also often drawn up by the Procureur, at the request of various Alderney States Committees, to control minor things such as the upkeep of roads, sewers, States' houses and other property, coastal erosion, water supplies, housing regulations, building and work permits, promotion of tourism, etc. These are paid for from the rates, congé (a tax of 5½% on real estate sales), the Impôt (the tax on alcohol and tobacco), harbour and airport dues, charges for services such as emptying cess-pits, pest control, etc. and any surplus from the tax revenue after Guernsey have taken out the costs of all of the services they administer. The States are also majority shareholders in the Alderney Electricity Company.

The Alderney Court has a Chairman and 6 other Jurats who retire at 70 unless their term of office is specially extended on an annual basis. Unlike in the other islands, they are NOT elected by the people, but appointed by the Home Office, after the Court's recommendation for a replacement has been approved by the President and the Lieutenant Governor. It has unlimited powers in civil matters, but very limited powers in criminal cases. More serious criminal cases and all appeals against judgement in either civil or criminal matters are dealt with by the Royal Court in Guernsey.

Alderney's South Cliffs

In this small book an attempt has been made to present historical, natural history and folklore information in the form which will help the walker, cyclist, or those who drive round the island, to appreciate and understand it, giving only such details as are relevant to the places passed on the way.

A 6in. map and a number of booklets about the flora and fauna of the island and various historical matters are obtainable from the Museum. Several of them are also available from the book, airport and paper shops. There are also some larger books on various aspects of the island's history available. The map may also be purchased at the Tourist Office.

The island has been divided into 15 "walks" which cover most of its $3^1/_2$ x $1^1/_2$ mile area. Each of these can be easily covered in a morning or afternoon in a leisurely stroll, giving the visitor plenty of time to explore, admire the views and take in the information about the place they are at at that moment. Many of them can equally well, but somewhat more rapidly, be covered on a bicycle. Few can be closely followed in car, since they have been designed to take the visitor to a number of places that cannot be seen from the roadways. Some of the coastal paths and tracks are not suitable for wheeled vehicles of any sort and, on a small number, vehicles are now forbidden, to prevent further erosion of the surface.

Several minibus tours and round the island boat trips are available and their drivers or pilots will give you much information about the places they pass. Those who hire a car may prefer to get out at various convenient points mentioned in the text and take all or part of the walks before returning to their vehicles. A quick tour by car is outlined at the end of the book.

Whichever option you take, please enjoy Alderney with its friendly people, peaceful atmosphere, excellent safe beaches, many splendid views, interesting military 'architecture', and often unique wildlife.

We hope you will come again.

WALKS IN ALDERNEY

Alderney's cliff and coastal paths offer the walker some spectacular views. Depending on the weather and where you are standing, you may see all of the other islands, with Jersey down on the horizon to the south, occasionally seen with the Corbière Lighthouse standing out on the right-hand end. In the afternoon, glinting sunlight reflects from several of the glasshouses on Guernsey, some 20 miles SW of Alderney. Between the two, from left to right, Sark and Brechou, Herm and Jethou can be seen, often as prominent black shapes against a light sky.

The French coast, some nine miles away at its nearest point, is usually visible from the east and south of the island. You may see as far south as the nuclear power station domes on the coast at Diellete, looking like two golf balls and the coast beyond, some 30-40 miles away. The huge array of buildings on top of the hill almost opposite Alderney is the Beaumont-Hague nuclear reprocessing plant, France's equivalent to Sellafield.

If you can clearly see the houses and fields on the Cap de la Hague, below this and to the left, it will probably rain next day. The Cape Lighthouse stands up like a pencil at the left-hand end of the promontory.

Alderney has a circumference of about 11 miles and it is quite possible for the active person to walk right round the island in a day. You will probably enjoy it more, see more of the beautiful views and the mass of wild flowers in season, if you take it in stages. In addition you won't wear yourself out!

The following suggestions offer walks which can easily be accomplished between meals. The approximate distance, and time taken for a leisurely stroll are given, and each is shown on its accompanying sketch map. Start and finish points are marked S & F. Compare this with the larger map of the island to fix your starting or finishing point. You can of course start from either end, but they have been planned so that there is in general more down-hill walking than up-hill.

If you have a car it may be easier to drive to the starting point, but you will sometimes have to return to recover the vehicle later, unless you can arrange for someone to drop you off there. Much of the island covered by these walks is not seen from the roadways either by car or on one of the island tours. Several, except those along the South coast cliff path, can be covered on a bicycle. Access to a number of the starting and finishing points may also be gained during the season, by the Riduna Bus Service. This was re-introduced in July 1994 after a gap of some 5-6 years. The bus leaves the Butes car park at 10, and 11am, 12 noon, 2, 3, and 4pm and covers a circular route taking in all of the eastern end of the island. This includes all of the swimming beaches and the camp site.

The fifteen walks can all be followed in a week's stay, several start and finish in town. They are divided up as follows;

Town Area;	- 1 walk
South coast cliffs;	- 4 sections
West coast;	- 2 sections
North coast including the Harbour;	- 3 sections
East coast;	- 1 section
Inland;	- 4 sections

1. The Town Area

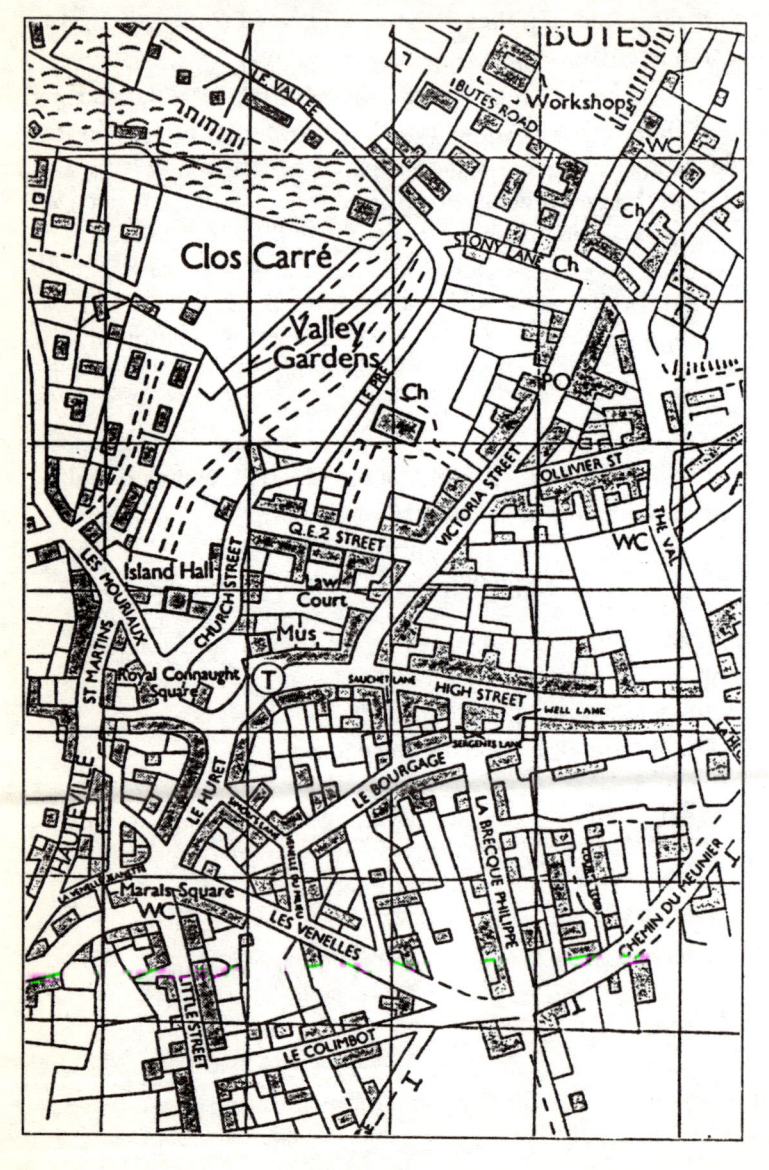

OUT AND ABOUT IN ALDERNEY

The town has grown up round the original settlement of the Bourgage and its adjacent Venelles or lanes. This was sited in a sheltered hollow, well supplied with water and close to the site of the earliest church and the open-air meeting place, near the present clock tower. The route suggested below gives some information about the various buildings and objects of interest passed along the way.

Start your walk at the Albert Gate in Victoria Street.

This gateway was erected by the Islanders in 1864, as a memorial to Prince Albert, husband of Queen Victoria, who had died in 1861. The original gates, bearing the initials VR and AP were damaged during the war and replaced in 1950. Walk down the driveway to the parish church of St. Anne. This, (originally re-ferred to as St. Ann), was erected in 1850 and consecrated by the Bishop of Winchester on August 21st.

The gift of the Rev. John Le Mesurier in memory of his parents, it cost just over £8,000. His father was the last of Alderney's Hereditary Governors. It is built of island stone with Caen stone finishings. The sculpture over the South porch represents the "Good Shepherd" with a lamb on his shoulder. Originally there were 660 seats for adults and 183 for children. Some 400 of these seats were in proprietary pews, whose owners paid an annual fee for them. The nearer the pulpit, the greater the fee!! The original stained glass windows were made by a Mr. Wailes of Newcastle, whilst on the north side a memorial window to Bishop Ryan and Rev. J.W.B. Robinson was installed in 1895. Rev. Ryan was Vicar of Alderney from 1834-46 when he was made Bishop of Mauritius. Rev. Robinson was appointed as Curate in 1850 to hold services at Braye for the Breakwater workmen. He then served as Vicar from 1851 to 1865. The modern west window depicts the children of all nations.

Gas lights were installed in 1859 and this lighting was used until the Second World War. The original heating was replaced in 1915 and again after the last war. The Germans had used the

Parish Church of St. Anne

church as a store, especially for barrels of wine, most of the pews had been removed and burnt, the bells had been removed from the tower to be melted down. One was still hanging outside the main door in a wooden gantry, another was found at the harbour when the island was relieved in 1945, the other four were later found in a field near Cherbourg in 1946 and returned to Alderney. They hung in wooden frames in the churchyard and were rung by ropes until they were recast and rehung in the belfry in 1953 on their original oak frames. They range in size from just over 4cwt. to just over 13cwt. Change ringing and the present band of Bell-Ringers were first started in 1979.

Outside the church;

On the north wall of the church you will see a bronze plaque commemorating the 45 Russian slave-workers who died and were buried in the Churchyard between 1941-45. More than 300 others were buried on Longis Common. A plan of their graves is kept in the States Office and the Museum. The bodies were removed by the War Graves Commission in the 1960s and reburied in a military cemetery in France.

Tombstones in the churchyard bear the names of many ancient island families as well as more recent immigrants from the Victorian era and later. Amongst them you will see memorials to two sailors killed by the Germans in the Great War when their troopship the SS *Pascall* was torpedoed by a submarine near the Casquets on 19th December 1916. Fortunately there were no troops on board at the time. The crew took to their boats which were then machine-gunned by the submarine killing two and wounding others.

Sapper George Onions was killed on 20th June 1945, shortly after the island was freed, whilst dismantling a booby-trapped mine. His grave, near the upper gateway, is still regularly tended and decorated with flowers by the islanders.

Enter by the South Doorway with its inner hallway, and use the door on your right.

Inside the church;

On the left in the nave is the font of Caen stone. The cross, the dove and the monogram IHS are carved on its pillars. The great west door is no longer used. Exposed to the prevailing south westerly winds it created a fierce draft in the church on occasions, the broad steps outside are of uneven height and therefore somewhat dangerous to use. Under the triple west window are six brasses to the Le Mesurier family.

On the wall in the north aisle is a list of the Priests, Rectors and Vicars of Alderney from 1490 to the present day. The north transept holds a Roll of Honour to Alderney's dead in two world wars and the standards of the British Legion. Suspended from the walls above are the old colours of the Royal Alderney Militia, a former British Legion standard and the Trinity House flag. The former chapel on this side, with its rose window and door to the Sacristy has been occupied since 1892 by the organ.

The carved oak screen or case surrounding it was made by local cabinet maker Mr. Batiste in 1906 and dedicated by the Bishop of Southampton on 8th May. Batiste completed and carved his name on it in the following year. The organ was upgraded in the 1970s and is now used several times a year for concerts by visiting organists, arranged by the Alderney Music Society, in addition to its regular use during services.

The pulpit at the junction of the nave and north transept is also of Caen stone. The bell rope suspended by it sounds the tenor bell. Pass along between the oak choir stalls with their elegant brass candle lamps. The semicircular apse has the altar rail across its diameter. The badge of St. Ann, a three-flowered lily stem, is in one of the windows above. The Lady Chapel, with its own altar, opens from the south transept. The south wall holds many plaques com-memorating island families and officers of the garrison who died here and, in a glass case, is a memorial to young Michael Wood. This is in the form of a model of the fishing boat Fleur de L'Ocean in which he died when it sank in The Race in July 1985. The south aisle has more commemorative plaques on its walls.

Parish Church interior at Christmas, about 1900

Today the seating, replaced after the war, holds about 320 people.

Leave the church by the path from the South doorway leading up to Queen Elizabeth II Street. This was originally called Rue des Héritiers when the Court of Heritage stood at the eastern end, then La Neuve Rue (New Street) when it was developed in the mid 1700s, but the name was changed to commemorate a visit of

H.M. the Queen in June 1978. Opposite you is the Courthouse, built by the island in 1849/51 at a cost of about £ 4,000, with the help of a loan from the Treasury (to be repaid over 12 years at £ 350 p.a.). This was handed over to the Crown on 14th November 1851. It contained the Courthouse (doubling as the States' Chamber), the Gaol, the Greffier's office and houses for the Greffier and Gaoler.

The States' Building, built 1851

Today it still houses the Court and States' Chamber, the members room, an office for the Clerk to the Court, and a large committee room in the central portion. The Police Station and gaol are on the right and several of the States offices on the left. The remaining States offices, including those of the President and the Clerk of the States are in St Anne's House opposite.

Over the door is the island crest. Recently, at the end of 1993, H. M. the Queen confirmed the grant to Alderney of a Coat of Arms by her great-grandfather. These had never been officially registered at the College of Heralds. A petition was made to her majesty by the Lt. Governor and the arms were then registered (in a very slightly modified form). Alderney is the first of the Channel Islands to have its official armorial bearings as opposed to an armorial seal. The word **Riduna**, below the crest, does not appear on the coat of arms. It is the old Roman name for the island.

The arms have always been incorporated in the island flag in the centre of the cross of St. George since it was originally granted in the reign of Edward VII. The flag is hoisted on all

Court Days, when the States are sitting and on other official occasions. It is also flown at half mast for the deaths of members of the Royal Family, the Lt. Governor, State's Members and prominent local people.

Turn right and opposite the end of the street you will see the 1720 house. Built about the time the street was formed, with the first island Courthouse, La Cour des Héritiers, rebuilt about 1740, at the opposite end, in what is now Victoria Street. Little of this building now remains. In earlier times the Court was held in the open air in the old churchyard. Turn left along Rue de L'Eglise, (Church Street) named from the site of the old parish church. On your left is the Masonic Hall, originally built in 1813/4 as the second Wesleyan Chapel in the island when the 1787 chapel became too small. After the fourth and present Chapel was built in 1851 where services were held in English, the French-speaking Methodists continued to hold their services here.

The stone building with the small terrace in front with a seat, was possibly built as either the Market House, about 1750 and 'demolished' about 1832 or more probably as a "Pest House" or isolation hospital. This spot is referred to in the Parish Registers of 1768 as Le Coignet des Malades, suggesting a "hospital". It later became the infant's school and is now a private residence.

On your right is the present 'Island Hall'. Rebuilt in 1763 by the Le Mesuriers as both their private residence and Government House, on the site of the former Lt. Governor, Captain Ling's house, which was built about 1660. It became purely the Government House when they built their mansion, Mouriaux House, just across the road on the far side, in 1777. The gardens originally went right down to the bottom of the town, to the Vallée pump and included The Terrace, now a public pleasure garden and the Valley Gardens, now run as a market garden, with the additional classroom of Ormer House School at the lower end. There is a spring here and a former pumphouse.

After the building of the Courthouse it became at various times an hotel, then a convent, to which was added in 1890 the large room on the right as you face it as a schoolroom. The Convent School then flourished here until the Second World War.

The German's turned it into their Soldatenheim or Soldier's Home, their equivalent of the English NAAFI. After the war it was repurchased by the States and used as offices. The Alderney Society Museum was set up in the basement in 1966, with the library then occupying the first floor and concert and committee rooms on the ground floor. Later the Youth Club occupied the basement after the Museum was moved to the Old School building. Today the Youth Club have their own premises on Butes.

The Island Hall is now the scene of most official receptions. Concerts are held in the Anne French Room. Various Committee meetings and the polling station at election times are here in the two front rooms. The Alderney Library is still on the first floor and the large school room is the scene of many island activities. Regular jumble sales, the Children's Playgroup, the Badminton Club, Keep-fit classes, the Alderney Drama Club presentations and the annual Christmas Pantomime. The monthly People's

The Island Hall, rebuilt 1763

Meetings, held by law before each sitting of the States, to allow the electorate to discuss the items in the Billet d'Etat, are also held here.

You are now in Royal Connaught Square, formerly known successively as St. Ann's Square and Royal Square, its name was changed in 1905 to commemorate the visit of the Duke of Connaught, son of Queen Victoria, as the tablet on the Vicarage wall informs you. Most of the buildings round this square were erected about 1800-1820. The present Vicarage was built at that time on the site of an earlier one. The Greffier then had his office in one of the smaller houses opposite and the Town Major lived here from about the same period. The Royal Connaught Hotel next to these was a private house, Seymour House, until the island was evacuated in 1940. It was also used for many years to house the boarders of the Convent School. The facade probably dates from about 1850. After the war it became an hotel and is now a residential care-home for the elderly.

The square originally had the island's principal stream running through it. This was put in a culvert and the square paved at an unknown date. On the southern side from the left were the old forge, the old Rose and Crown Pub and the large house, now bearing a heritage plaque was, from soon after the last war, the residence of author T.H. White. An eccentric character, he built a Greek theatre in the garden. There is a bust of a Roman Emperor on top of the wall. White is perhaps best remembered for his book *The Once and Future King* which was turned into the highly successful musical *Camelot*.

The tree in the iron railings at the side of the square is an Indian Chestnut from Windsor Great Park. Its creamy flowers come in July, about six weeks later than the ordinary Horse Chestnuts. One was planted here by Princess Elizabeth in June 1949, to replace the Horse Chestnut formerly in the road on the other side of the Island Hall entrance. This was planted by the

Duke of Connaught in 1905, and had recently been cut down as an obstruction to traffic. The original Indian tree died some time later and this one was sent from Windsor to replace it.

Leave the square by the road to the left of the Island Hall. Les Mouriaux House on your left bears a heritage plaque marking it as the former residence of the island's hereditary governors. Opposite is the recent States development of Alexandra Court, small houses for local people, opened by Princess Alexandra in June 1990. At the top of this short street on the right is the German water tower. Until recently used as one of the pumping stations for the island's water supply. It was up to that time also used by the farmers to fill their water carts to take to the cattle in the fields.

Mouriaux House about 1950; built 1777

The Alderney Pottery is a few yards further on, on the right. Offering a range of locally produced pottery, paintings and homespun and woven woollen goods, it also provides refreshments for most of the day. The Gazebo now forming part of the Pottery wall was probably built by the Le Mesuriers to give them a view (no longer to be seen) of their ships entering the harbour. Retrace your steps past Mouriaux House and walk along St. Martins on the right.

Many of the houses in this street retain their Georgian glazing at least to the upper windows. Those on the right are built back into the bank and have their gardens level with the first floor. This late 18th century development then housed many of the richer class in Alderney, including several Jurats

French pottery horseman on roof of Les Chevaliers

and farmers. The house and garden of one John Pezet here was bought by the Collecteurs des Pauvres (Poor Law Board) of the States on 13th June 1789, "for the erection of an 'hospital' for the poor" (i.e. an Almshouse). A small cobbled lane on the left has the Alderney Fire Station on its corner and leads back to Royal Connaught Square. Les Chevaliers on the right opposite is a particularly good example of the buildings of the time, formerly with four French pottery mounted horsemen ornamenting the roofs, only one of which now survives intact.

At the next junction, Hauteville with similar houses goes straight on, but turn left at Le Coin des Écailles, a short twisting street originally named from the stile, or gap in the hedge, leading out of Marais Square. In Victorian times one of the island's public pumps was on the corner nearest the square. The short Rue de la Fontaine leads to La Venelle Jeannette, known as La Mare Jean Bot in the 16th Century (and still so-called by many older islanders) back into Marais Square, also known earlier as La Place des Vaches (Cow Square).

This interesting square was repaved and the huge abreuvoir publique or public cattle trough erected in 1882. Well into the present century a man was employed to keep the trough filled and to clean up the manure each day. It was originally marshy, as the name implies. The stream then flowed across it to Royal Square and on down to Le Vallée, (whose name comes from the Le Vallez family who owned the land here at one time and is not a misuse of French gender). The women washed their clothes there, probably at the bottom of Little Street, then known as La Rue des Vaches. The name La Petite Rue dates from at least 1770, but in the 1851 Census it is referred to as Cow-pat Lane. The site of the Victorian public pump, one of the principal sources of water for the town on the corner outside the Marais Hall Hotel is now only marked by a steel manhole over the well. The pump was removed in the 1960s when the town was fully equipped with a mains water supply.

The square was also the principal source of water for the earliest settlement. This was built on the higher ground just above it to the east, around the Bourgage. It had several gateways leading onto the Blayes, the communal

Marais trough with cattle about 1935

agricultural land, from the streets leading out of it and cattle were brought here daily to drink. Most of the farmhouses were in the central area of the old town, many built back into the slopes of the hollow, with their gardens level with the upper storey. The entrances to the small farmyards were alongside and many of these now only exist as gateways or garages.

The Marais Hall Hotel is one of the older hostelries in the town and offers excellent bar lunches and restaurant facilities. Their Sunday lunch is very good value. Around the turn of the century a ginger beer factory was established alongside. It is now the Alderney Motors garage.

Make a short diversion up the street on the left of the Marais Hall, La Trigale. An access gate to the Grande Blaye was at the top of this street. Here you will see the only surviving example in Alderney of the Norman arched doorway, still quite frequently seen in old Guernsey houses. These low rounded arches had two courses. The first, of three shaped stones, was surmounted by a second of either seven or, as here, fourteen stones. This one is considerably older than the house and might have been inserted at a later date.

Marais Pump 1946

Return to Marais Square and take the turning on the right, Little Street. Public toilets are sited on the corner. A few yards up on the right is a short lane known as Le Coignet, another of the original access points to the Blaye. A public washing place was sited somewhere about here in earlier times. The houses in this street are also built back into the sloping bank and have their gardens above the first floor level. Several were farmhouses at one time. On the left further up is Le Colimbot, formerly Le Culi'bot, now bearing a street name plate "Colin Bot". He was a Jurat in 1517 who probably owned the land here, his wife was the Jeanne Bot of the little, formerly marshy, lane at Marais Square.

Take this turning and follow the road lined with both old and more recent houses to the triple junction. The road straight ahead is Le Chemin du Meunier, the Miller's Road and led to one of Alderney's two windmills, formerly at the far end. The 'New Mill' was built here in 1560 by the Le Ber family and paid a tithe to the Crown of £10 a year. Long derelict, but still with its weather vane in the shape of a fish on top, it was finally demolished, as a potential hazard to aircraft, in the 1960s when the airport runway was lengthened. This road has some of the larger farmhouses, built in Channel Island fashion with their gable ends against the roadway. There were two more gateways to the Grande Blaye along here, one opposite La Brêque Philippe and the other at the far end at La Hêche. Alderney's first power station, in a large corrugated iron shed, was erected along the sandy track on the right there in 1936. This building was only demolished and replaced by a new store building in 1994. Brêque and Hêche both signify gateways. The one by the mill had a keeper who used to charge 2 sous for admission to the Blaye after sunset.

The gates were there to keep the cattle out of the cultivated land and were maintained at the expense of the land owners. Turn left at the end and the short La Hêche brings you to the junction of Le Val, La Grande Rue (High Street) and Longis Road. On the opposite corner, the brown-painted wall is all that remains of the Scottish Presbyterian Church built in 1840. It ceased to be used as a church about 1900 and was turned into a Roller-skating rink and dance hall. Known as 'The Rink' it later doubled as the cinema of the Alderney Picture Palace Company from the 1920s. It was one of the first buildings in Alderney to be electrified in 1936. The Germans turned it into a luxury cinema for their troops. Their projector continued to be used after the war and the building became 'The Lyceum'. It ceased to be used as a cinema in 1958, was the subject of an arson attack in 1969 and was finally demolished in 1977. Part of the original church still remains in Lyceum House.

Turn left into High Street or La Grande Rue. On the right is the Jubilee Home, a hospital for the elderly and infirm, erected to commemorate Queen Victoria's Golden Jubilee in 1887. Administered until 1948 by the Poor Law Board, since the war it has

The Rink, about 1920

Sauchet Lane, about 1910

been the old people's home. It is still run by the States of Alderney with residents paying according to their means. An extension has been built behind, where up to a dozen better off elderly residents can pay for a small bed-sitter with nursing care and meals provided if required. A few yards away take the very short Well Lane (Venelle des Puits or Pisse), on the left. This originally had a public well and connected the oldest settlement of the town, along Le Bourgage, with the 18th century Grande Rue. Along the Bourgage on the left is the other end of La Brêque Philippe, with Venelle du Serjent or Sergeant's Lane almost opposite. A house and land here was in former times the perquisite of the Serjent, a Court Official who received the use of it as part of his salary. Despite the antiquity of the settlement in this part of the town, none of the surviving older buildings seem to date before the eighteenth century in their present form.

The next lane is Sauchet Lane, the site of former Watercress beds from which it got its name, with the second of the town pumps at its lower end. This too was removed about 1960. The large pump handle can be seen in the Museum. Between the two lanes in the High Street is the Salvation Army Citadel. Built in the 1830s as the third Wesleyan Chapel, for the 'Primitive Methodists', it became the Salvation Army HQ when the island Corps was formed on May 5th 1881. The house at the top of Sauchet Lane, where you are now standing has its ground floor wall rounded on the corner to facilitate the turning of carts. At the end of Le Bourgage is the oldest part of the town. The lane on the left, Venelle du Milieu, signifies the centre of the settlement. None of the earlier houses now remain here, only their blank walls on the right with some bricked up doorways showing. The turning on the right is the Venelle Simon, an old island family name pronounced Simmo. Follow it down to Le Huret.

Derived from the Norse word *haugr*, meaning a mound, this was the island's traditional open air meeting place. Marais Square is now on your left, but turn right past the present Rose and Crown pub. Almost opposite 'The Old Corner House' was formerly another pub of that name. The single storied building on the corner just beyond was the old island Forge.

The triangular space between here and the bottom of the High Street was the traditional open air meeting place of the islanders. Long before the houses were built the adult population assembled here to decide on the

Engraving. Le Huret 1830

start of the spring and autumn vraic (seaweed) gathering seasons. Arguments took place about the suitability of the weather and tides, but when all was settled and the time appointed almost the whole island took part in gathering, carting and drying the seaweed to fertilise the Blayes. Entries in the School Log Books in autumn and spring each year from the 1860s, note a poor attendance for several consecutive days due to the seaweed gathering. Similarly at harvest time, custom decreed that the date for cutting the corn was set by the Governor after a meeting here. The church bell was then rung to signify the start and the fields on the island were cut and the sheaves put up in stooks to dry. When all was cut and ready, carting could begin. This was carried out in a prescribed order of the various fields, with the tithes for church and crown being carefully separated and counted as the sheaves were carried to the barns. When all was completed the bell was rung again to signify that the inhabitants could now put their cattle and sheep on the Blayes to graze the stubble until the spring ploughing began.

As recently as the end of the Great War, all important announcements were still made here. As an example the Sheriff, (another Court Official) read the proclamation of the end of that war from a platform erected here in 1918.

On the Vicarage wall beside this spot is a plaque commemorating the visit of HM The Queen in July 1957. She planted a tree in the middle of the junction in the spot formerly occupied by a gas lamp. You can still see the circle of cobblestones replaced after the tree was demolished by a vehicle in the 1960s.

To the right of this plaque is the entrance gateway to the old school building, now the Museum. Alderney was one of the first places in the British Isles to have a free school, erected by Governor John Le Mesurier in 1790. Poor people were educated free, those who could afford it paid 3d. (just over 1p) a week. It was also the last place in the British Isles to introduce compulsory education in 1924, after nearly 40 years of almost annual debate on whether to do so or not. It was divided into two by a partition, there was a fireplace at each end and the Boys and Girls entered by separate entrances, still in use, into a passage where they could hang their coats. The daily log books of the boys and girls schools from 1862 to 1908 can be seen in the Museum. The building was used as a military hospital during the Great War, and the school finally moved to the new building at Newtown in 1969.

Museum entrance with Victorian Royal Arms

The Victorian Royal Arms mounted on the wall were probably brought to the island and used at the Breakwater on Queen Victoria's visit in 1854. They were found after the Second World War on a scrap heap in the island and were later given to the Museum and refurbished by the curator in the 1980s. Alderney's Victorian Pillar Box and one of the traditional old London style Telephone Boxes, (but painted yellow), stand outside the gate.

Enter the wooden gates to the left of the phone box and you are in the old churchyard. There was a church here from at least the eleventh century, possibly on the site of St. Vignalis chapel from the 6th century. Before that, the rounded, elevated form of the site above a flowing stream, is suggestive of a pagan holy place.

All that remains of the former Parish Church is the clock tower which was added to it in 1767

Le Mesurier tombs in Old Churchyard

after the church had been extended by the addition of a side chapel and gallery in 1761. The clock dates from 1808. The remainder of the original church was demolished in 1851 after the new Parish Church was completed. Inside the former chancel are the tombs of several of the Le Mesurier Governors. Captain Ling's tomb dating from 1679 can be seen on the left side of the churchyard close to the Vicarage wall. He was Lt. Governor of Alderney from 1657 until his death. Other tombstones bear the names of old island families, most of whom can still be found in the island.

Leave the churchyard, which, together with the Vicarage garden originally ran down to the stream, by the gap in the wall by the memorial seat and you are at the Museum entrance.

This small museum is well worth a visit. It contains an interesting display of island life over the centuries and includes a number of relics of the German Occupation from 1940-45. Many of the books and booklets about Alderney history and natural history are on sale here. The Museum, except for the Administrative Assistant and the cleaner, is staffed entirely by volunteers and is open during the season from 10-12 and 2-4 daily except Sunday afternoon.

After leaving the Museum by the arched gateway turn left. You are now in High Street and in about 100 yards will find the top of Victoria Street on your left. This junction used to be known as Blaggud's Corner. It was also the site of the principal garland suspended across the street on

Coronation Inn sign

High Street about 1910

May Day, beneath which the inhabitants used to dance a traditional dance called Le Beau Laurier. The Maypole was not apparently used in Alderney. On your right notice the Coronation Inn. This was first opened in 1953 and the sign commemorates the fact that the Queen is also Duke (not Duchess) of Normandy. In the Channel Islands the loyal toast is drunk to "The Queen, our Duke". A few yards beyond the junction on the left is the Campania Inn, one of the island's oldest suviving pubs. Run by the Hammond family from the 1890s until a few years ago. Bar snacks and restaurant facilities are now offered. The portions are man-sized and excellent.

Turn left into Victoria Street and you will be back at your starting point in another 200 yards or so. In this part of the street there are a number of restaurants. On your left immediately is "The Courier", an Italian restaurant. Ingrid's Cafe almost opposite has a wonderful selection of cakes. A few yards further down on the same side is Nellie Gray's. This was formerly York House, a family run guest house. The house now offers full restaurant facilities, whilst behind it, up the alleyway, is a large garden. Here "Nellie's Garden" is run separately as an outdoor bistro with, in addition, a large covered area. Further down the road still, the large house that lays well back from the road, almost opposite the Riduna Stores is called "North Star". On the northern gable end is a large compass star in pargetting. This is best seen from the Albert Mews in Ollivier Street a few yards down on the right. The Albert House Inn on its corner, offers restaurant facilities and also excellent bar lunches whose portions are enormous. Opposite this is the Chez André Hotel, formerly Andover House the residence of Capt. Marriette, Alderney's Postmaster just before the war, when the Riduna Stores alongside it formed the island's Post Office and chemists. Now a colonel, from 1949 to 1960 he was the first Chairman of Alderney's newly constituted Court. The bar on the left offers bar snacks, whilst the hotel provides full meals in the evening and an excellent Sunday Lunch menu.

Below the church gate where you started your walk, on the left you will find St. Catherine's, a house with another heritage plaque. This one commemorates island born Sir Henry Gauvain, a pioneer of chest surgery at the Lord Mayor Treloar Hospital in Alton, Hampshire. Further down, the pale green painted Grosnez House was once the residence of Judge Barbenson and the Midland Bank attached to it was once the Riduna Club, formed during the Boer War as a reading room and club where war news could be exchanged. The War Memorial in its garden is opposite. It was given to the island by the Judge in 1920. The Georgian House on the left was formerly Riou's Commercial Hotel. It ceased to offer accommodation a few years ago and is now only a Restaurant and pub. The bar area offers excellent snacks or you can eat in the restaurant. During the summer there is a bar and barbecue in the garden behind which is very popular. Almost opposite the Georgian, the bakery offers sandwiches and pasties in addition to the usual bread and cakes. Finally the last building in the street is Gannet's Café, also with an outside terrace and a licence for drinks.

On the wall bounding their terrace is a plaque commemorating the visit of Queen Victoria in 1854, in

Re-enactment in Alderney Week 1990, of Queen Victoria naming Victoria Street in 1854

whose honour the street was renamed. Formerly the Rue Grosnez, (Big Nose). It was at an earlier date still, known as La Rue des Sablons, (Sandy Road).

The elegant house facing you in Les Rochers, which looks up the full length of the street was built about 1800. The residence of Judge Mellish at the turn of the century, after the last war it was given to the Catholic church for use as the Presbytery. It has recently been sold and the priest lives in a smaller house behind. The cobbled lane on your left known locally as Stony Lane but properly called La Route des Marcheurs, leads down to the former public pump and cattle trough for the lower end of town, in Le Vallée. This lovely tree-lined valley with a flowing stream leads down to the sea at Platte Saline

Queen's Birthday parade on Butes, 1885. 2nd Bttn. Gordon Highlanders and the Royal Alderney Artillery Militia

If you continue a few yards further to the left, past the fourth, last and present Methodist Chapel, built in 1851, the Belle Vue Hotel offers good bar snacks and full restaurant facilities. It

OUT AND ABOUT IN ALDERNEY

also has an outside garden where bar snacks are served in the summer.

At the top of this short street you are on Butes. Once the principal parade ground for the island militia and garrison, as the name implies it was in earlier days used as an archery practice ground. The stone building on the left was built in the late 1700s as an arsenal for the militia to store their cannon, powder and shot. In the 1880s it was turned into a military hospital, and now houses the island's public works department. Built onto it in the last few years is the pavilion and changing rooms of the Alderney Cricket Club.

Riduna Bus, 1994

Beyond is the Island's Butes Centre. HQ of the Youth Club and also intended as a Day Centre for the Elderly. It was opened by the Queen on her visit in 1989. There is a lovely view of the harbour and much of the northern and eastern parts of the island from here. The town is spread out on the slopes behind you.

The Grand Hotel, 1938

OUT AND ABOUT IN ALDERNEY

The Grand Hotel on Fire, 1981

The large derelict area to the west of the Butes Centre was the site of Alderney's premier hotel, the Grand Hotel. Built in 1937 it was totally destroyed by fire in March 1981 and has never been rebuilt.

For several centuries Butes has been the scene of many a military parade and exercises for both the Alderney Militia and the various units of the British army who have been in garrison here. Although both are now gone, it is still the place for many island activities and ceremonies. Princess Elizabeth addressed the people of the island from beneath an awning erected here in 1949. Many of the Alderney Week functions also take place here. The bus to the eastern parts of the island now starts from the right-hand side of the car park.

2. The South Coast
Walk 2. The Giffoine to the top of Little Street.
(2^1/$_2$ Miles, 2-3 hours to enjoy it).

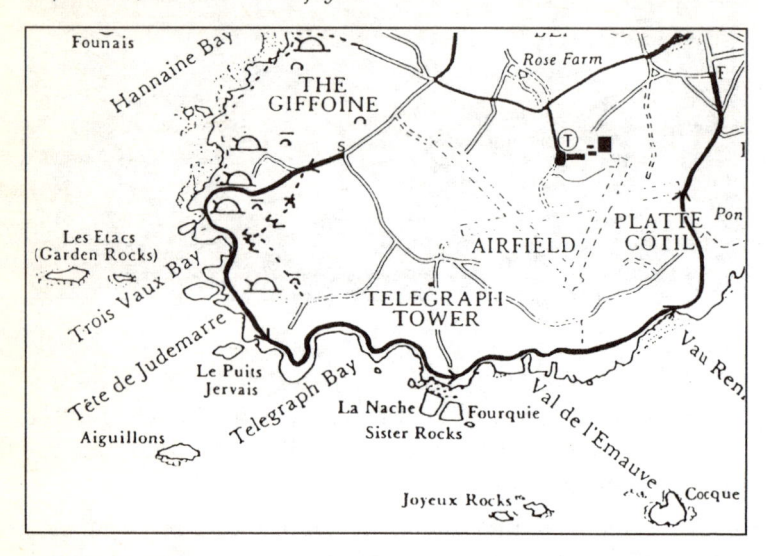

The word Giffoine is derived from an old Norman-French word meaning "Land used for hunting". It was part of the Crown or common lands until much of them was divided amongst the inhabitants in 1830.

Your walk starts from the end of the tarmac road which runs south from the corner of Le Grand Val (passing the Airport entrance) and the road coming up from Fort Tourgis.

At this point the old 25ft. gravelled military road running along the south side of the island, between the airfield and the cliffs is on your left. Straight ahead is another sandy track, improved by the Germans during the war for access to Batterie Anne, one of their largest defensive positions. Follow this. On your left is the valley of Trois Vaux, leading down to the sea to the top of a low cliff above a tiny bay formerly used by smugglers. On your right are a number of German bunkers at intervals and between two of them about 100 yards from your starting point the ruins of a former brick kiln. The track soon divides; take the right hand branch, bear left as the gravelled track turns and you

Brig. Snow with captured German officers at "The Guns" on Le Giffoine, on the liberation of Alderney, 16th May 1945

will come upon more bunkers and four large gun emplacements. These were used by the Germans to house 15cm naval gun turrets removed from old warships. They had a range of 22,000m (about 13 miles). The whole area is now a honeycomb of underground bunkers and tunnels and accordingly, in the main unfit for extensive cultivation.

Walk down the grassy track to the right of the gunsite by the car parking area and in front of you, from late January until the end of the summer you will see a site rarely seen from inhabited land, a **Gannet** Colony. Straight ahead on a group of rocks known as Les Etacs or Les Gardiens, (locally called the 'Garden Rocks') is a breeding colony of some 2-3,000 pairs of these magnificent birds with a 6ft wingspan. During the spring and summer the rocks turn white with their manure. This is usually washed off in the winter storms which, on occasion, break right over the rocks. If the wind is from the SW you will be almost deafened by the clattering of their beaks and a strong smell will reach your nose. Hundreds of birds are usually circling overhead or resting on the sea and skeins of a dozen or more will often be seen flying in line a few feet above the water, returning from their fishing grounds to feed the hungry youngsters. The rocks got their name centuries ago from the fact that they guard the entrance to the Swinge, the dangerous tidal passage between Alderney and Burhou.

Beyond is the Casquets Lighthouse, now completely automatic and controlled from the Alderney Lighthouse it flashes continuously day and night. five flashes every thirty seconds and the mirrors, contrary to the usual custom, rotate in an anticlockwise direction. It now has a range of about 28 miles in clear weather. The deep note of its compressed air foghorn has recently been replaced by a high pitched electronic beep.

The Casquets Lighthouse was first built in 1724, when it consisted of three towers of equal height, in each of which a coal fire was maintained in the lantern, These were replaced by a ring of eight paraffin burners in 1790 and a clockwork operated revolving mechanism giving one flash every 15 seconds was fitted to each in 1818. These had to be wound by hand every 1$^1/_2$ hours. A bell was then used as a fog signal. The height of the towers was raised by 30ft in 1854 and the lamps were by then of 184,000 candle power giving three slow flashes every half minute. They had a range of about 10-12 miles. In 1877 the light was changed to a single petrol vapour lamp with a quick flashing signal 5 times every 30 seconds, in the NE tower which was again made taller.

First electrified in 1952, the light, which is 120ft above sea level, then had over 2.8 million candle power and a range of 14 miles. The Casquets have been the scene of many wrecks both before and since the erection of the lighthouse. Many fishing and cargo vessels have perished there, as well as several naval and passenger vessels. HMS *Albion*, a frigate was wrecked here about 1709, HMS *Dragon*, a 38-gun Man-of War in 1711 and HMS *Victory*, in 1744. A 110-gun first-rater, the largest ship in the British navy at the time, she sank with the loss of 1,100 men. There were no survivors. A very large canon, 9 feet long, from HMS *Dragon* was brought up in 1994 and will be displayed in Alderney when it has been conserved.

The LSWR steamer *Stella* was lost there in 1899 with the loss of 105 lives. 120 men, women and children were rescued. Most

Wreck of Tanker Constantia S *on Casquets, 23rd January 1967*

recently *Constantia* S, a Greek tanker of 8,700 tons was wrecked here in January 1967. She was carrying a cargo of fresh water from Rotterdam to Gibraltar. Twenty of the crew were rescued by the Trinity House Launch *Burhou* which was then stationed in Alderney, the remaining ten men were picked up from their lifeboat by the railway steamer *Sarnia*. The Captain was picked up from the rocks by helicopter. She broke up and sank some time later.

The legends of the Casquets are part of Alderney's Folk lore. Tradition places the sinking of *La Blanche Nef*, the "White Ship" here in 1120 with the loss of Prince William heir to Henry I, although this has long been established as occuring off Barfleur.

Long ago, one of the Seigneurs of Jersey, a warrior and a giant of a man, had a beautiful wife. A wealthy Auregnais, out fishing in Jersey waters, saw her walking on the shore, whilst her husband was off fighting in France. They fell in love and used to meet often.

One day, whilst with her lover, the lady heard that her husband was on his way home, so they got into the fishing boat and sailed for Alderney. When the husband arrived, he found his wife gone and the boat almost over the horizon. His helmet had magic powers and he threw it violently after them, at the same time laying a curse on them, that they should never reach land.

The helmet *(or Casque)* carried a great distance and fell over the fishing boat. It turned into the dangerous helmet-shaped rocks which have ever since been feared by all passing ships.

To the right of the Casquets, between them and the island of Burhou is the haystack-shaped rock named Ortac. This is another **Ganne**t colony and also has a legend.

The name itself derives from the time of the Norse pirates who invaded the islands in the 8-9th centuries, and means 'Thor's Rock'. There is a legend of a cave beneath the rock known as The Oven, where thousands of sea-birds nest. They are reputed to throw their eggs out of the nest to smash them if a human intrudes, sweeping them off the ledges with their wings. It is also reputedly the home of a spirit of wind and water (perhaps the Norse god Thor?) to which fishermen, well into the 19th century, used to stop and drink a toast as they passed the rock.

To the right again is a long area of emergent reefs from the Renonquet, scene of the loss of Britain's fastest warship, the turbine driven torpedo boat HMS *Viper*, in 1901 with no loss of life, past the bird sanctuary islands of Little Burhou and Burhou to the Nannels reef, scene of several shipwrecks including the 2,500 ton MV *Arma*s in 1973. Her crew were rescued by two Sea King helicopters from the RFA vessel *Engadin*e which happened to be near the Casquets, 13 from the ship and 9 from the nearby rocks. One man was drowned. Below about half tide level, the square black box-shape of her engine can still be seen from where you are standing. To the right again the largest flat-topped rock in the Grosse Rock. This too has its legend.

The White Bull of Grosse Rock is said to haunt the road from Clonque to Platte Saline and up Le Petit Val to the trough in Ladysmith, where he goes to drink twice a year when the sea clears the rock at the Great Tides. A young girl washing clothes at the stone lavoiret known locally as the doüit, (Les Doüits is being corrupted to Ladysmith) saw the animal drinking and spoke to it. The bull answered; "Those that walk in the sea are never dry; and those that drink of salt water are always thirsting". She followed it down to the beach where it trotted across the shingle, struck the Grosse rock with its horn, the rock opened and the bull went inside, the girl followed and was never seen again. The white stockings she had been washing were washed ashore by the incoming tide.

Jutting out from Alderney in your line of view is the offshore islet of La Clonque with its Victorian Fort and Causeway. More of this in a later walk.

Retrace your steps a few yards and on your left the first tiny bay with its near vertical cliffs is home to a colony of **Fulmars**. You will probably see them gliding on their stiffly held wings on the air currents in this bay. From above the brownish circular markings on top of their wings are clearly seen. You might also see **Ravens** tumbling in their strange courtship flight in the spring and the occasional **Marsh Harrier** flying in from the sea to spend a day or two round the airport.

In the spring this part of the cliffs is carpeted with **Gorse** and pink **Thrift**. If you are here on a day when the offshore stacks are surrounded with sea mist their yellow and pink showing against the background of mist with only the tops of the stacks showing is a truly memorable sight. Now follow the track across the slope of the hillside to the left of Les Etacs down the steep incline to Trois Vaux Bay. At one time this was a favourite landing place for smugglers to leave their cargo and a flight of wooden steps led down to the beach. The stream from the valley forms a small waterfall here. Cross the stream and continue up the steep track along the cliff edge to the Tête de Judemarre. This was the former site of a 16th or 17th century Watchtower, manned during times of trouble by the Militia or the Army, and before that a signal beacon. The name probably derives from 'Hougue-ès-Mât', a 'mound with a beacon' or Beacon Hill.

If you are here in later spring or early summer the sides of the valley behind you are usually carpeted with white **Ox-eye**

Daisies. There are more remains of German gun mountings here, this time Ack-Ack and machine guns. Follow the path along the cliff through the heather. The next bay is called Le Puits Jervais, 'Jervais Well'. It was the scene of another wreck in 1975. The 1,500 ton Shell tanker *Point Law* drove straight in here in a gale one summer's night and landed with her bows on the small beach. She had a crew of 12 and was fortunately in ballast. Some of the crew scrambled ashore. The St. Peter Port lifeboat attended and, as it got light, managed to transfer six of the men to the lifeboat, one at a time, using two rubber dinghies. The lifeboat crew later received several bravery awards for their efforts in hazardous conditions. The Alderney Fire Brigade Cliff Rescue Team got some of the men up the cliff, after dealing with a gorse fire caused by the distress flares. The remaining three crew were lifted off the ship by helicopter which also lifted three of the firemen off the cliff. Attempts some time later to tow the tanker off failed. She broke into three parts, disintegrated and the remains were sold for scrap.

Wreck of Tanker Point Law *15th July 1975*

The next bay is one of Alderney's favourite, but less accessible swimming spots, Telegraph Bay. It has caves, rock pools and a lovely sandy beach. Called Fouleur Bay in olden

Telegraph Bay

times, it came by its present name after the erection of a semaphore signal station linking Alderney with Guernsey and Jersey via a relay station on Sark was erected by the Prince de Bouillon in 1795. This was replaced in 1811 by another signal mast on top of the Telegraph Tower, built a little further on. A submarine telegraph cable linking Weymouth to Alderney via Portland and then on to Guernsey was opened in 1858. It reached Alderney at the north-eastern side of the island near Château à L'Etoc, ran overland to a hut on the cliff near the site of the old signal mast and entered the sea in the bay. You can still see a small concrete junction house and part of the cable towards the bottom of the cliff. Sometimes after a storm the cable is exposed running across the beach and into the sea. The cable was frequently out of action through storm damage, often for months, before it could be restored and in 1895 another signal mast was erected here. The cut-off stump of the wooden mast and the concrete blocks holding the stay wires can still be seen in the short turf and bare ground on the headland to the west of the bay.

Follow the bay round until you come to the railing at the top of a long flight of steps, about 250 in all. These lead down to the beach and were erected in Victorian times. Despite several repair works carried out in recent years by the Alderney Junior Militia and visiting Army units, the bottom section gets continually washed away in winter storms. The access to the beach for the last twenty feet or so has to be negotiated by the help of a stout rope. This descent is now only for the very active. If you ignore the notice warning you of the danger of this path, make sure you don't get cut off from the bottom of the steps by the rising tide. At high water the bay is filled to the bottom of the cliffs which are far too crumbling and dangerous to climb.

For the naturalist these cliffs hold much of interest. **Prostrate Broom**, **Thrift** and **Ox-eye Daisies** clothe them with yellow, pink and white in late spring, interspersed with the small royal-blue flowers of **Sheep's-bit**. The Prostrate Broom is quite a rare plant in UK where it is only found in W. Wales and the extreme SW of England. Parasitic on its roots is the **Greater Broomrape**, present along here in some quantity. The Yellow-Brown flower stems, about 9in high and 1in. diameter remain for months after flowering in May. This too is quite rare in UK nowadays, being badly affected by herbicide sprays. In the bare earth bank by the railings at the top of the steps look for the many small holes made by solitary boring bees. On a warm afternoon they are often busy carrying nectar into their holes to store for the grubs to feed on when the eggs hatch. If you are lucky you might also see some **Ravens** tumbling over the cliffs and circling the bay above you here.

Carry on along the cliff-edge path. The concrete plinth in the field on your left was the mounting point for a German Radio mast. About 300yds inland stands the circular bulk of the Telegraph Tower. This was designed for the Admiralty in 1811, by Peter Mulgrave the Government Inspector of Telegraphs, to replace the former signal mast. It has three floors, each with its fireplace, for the telegrapher's accomodation. It fell into disuse after the electric telegraph cable came into use. In 1874 it passed to the War Office and was let to various people as a residence. About the turn of the century it served as an isolation hospital for a case of cholera. Again rented out by the War Department between the wars, it was purchased by the States of Alderney in 1950 with other crown lands. It continued as a rather primitive residence into the 60s, but when the last tenant died was abandoned. Derelict for many years, in 1994 it was again leased and at the time of writing is well on the way to being turned back into a pleasant habitation. The plot of land which belongs with it is marked on the four corners by WD marker stones. Along this part of the walk, by now, several aircraft will probably have taken off or landed on the airfield behind you. The first view of Alderney for the late spring visitor is often from an Aurigny plane coming in over the Garden Rocks and seeing the **Gannets** on and around it who completely ignore the aircraft, followed almost immediately by the pink, white and yellow of Alderney's wild flowers on the cliffs.

Continue along the cliff-edge path. At times this is a little hard to follow for it is now not greatly frequented. The lookout on the southernmost point of Alderney is another German defence post, offering spectacular views of the cliffs in both directions. All of the other Channel Islands can be seen along most of this walk, and a long section of the French coast to the left. Jersey is straight in front of you, its northern cliff face showing as a dark line down on the horizon. On the right hand end if the light is right you can pick out the Corbière Lighthouse. To the right and much nearer lies Sark. The smaller island close to it is Brechou. Further right again lies Herm with Jethou to its right. The largest island is of course Guernsey. In the afternoon sun you will frequently pick out the reflections of light from its many glasshouse spans and the chimneys of the power station at St. Sampsons.

You have now reached the Val L'Emauve. Mauve means 'Seagull'. At this point a high waterfall from the tiny stream above falls over the cliff. The curious rock formation like a seat with a vertical drop into the narrow bay below is called the Chaise à L'Emauve or the Lover's Chair. Sometimes also called

Engraving of Naftel Sketch. "View from the Lover's Chair"

the Lover's Leap several legends surround it. One concerns Jacquine, the beautiful daughter of a former Governor of Alderney, who fell in love with a young farmer. Her father forbade the match and wanted her to marry a wealthy Guernsey business man. She refused and used to meet her lover here. Finally her father relented and agreed to their marriage, but on their wedding morning she disappeared in her bridal gown. After the whole island had turned out to search for her, her bridegroom thought to go to their trysting place. She had slipped over the cliff and was on the shingle below. He got help and she was brought up but died later that night.

In another legend the son of a Governor of Guernsey had fallen in love with an Alderney peasant girl and used to visit her often. Someone informed his father of the liaison and the father took ship with some of his servants and sailed for Alderney. They found the lovers at this spot, who, rather than be separated, leapt off the cliff to their deaths on the rocks below. When their bodies were recovered they were so tightly entwined that they could not be separated. They were buried together nearby and the father returned home.

On the cliffside to the right of the tiny bay as you look out to sea is another unusual plant **Sea Purslane**. This usually grows in marshy sand on the edges of saltwater pools. Here, at its only site in Alderney, it grows in some profusion on the cliff face and on a small level patch above it, about 100ft above the water. The track now runs a little inland behind the Lover's Chair and up a steep path. The ground is often moist here and, in bare patches amongst the heather, between late April and early July, you may see clumps of the lovely pink flowers of the semi-parasitic plant **Lousewort**. Continue along the narrow track and, after some spectacular rock outcrops on the edge of the cliff, quite low at this point, the track rises and you come to a more open area with a seat. Rest awhile and admire the view. The remains of a jetty can be seen at the foot of the cliffs some way ahead and beyond again a view of the Hanging Rocks. We will come to both these features on another walk. The cliffs are not quite so steep here and for about a quarter of a mile in front of the seat the track is easy. It passes a small quarry on its seaward side. Inside this quarry, known for at least 40 years, is a colony of the rare Royal **Fern**. A tall fern which has formed a large clump, with many "flowering" stems in June-August. It never seems to have produced more plants either here or anywhere else in the island.

Another 100 yards or so brings you to a rocky bank. Either side of the path if you are here in the morning, on a sunny day from May to July you should see the **Spotted Rock Rose**. Another Alderney speciality, it has small primrose-yellow petals with brown spots. This little annual plant drops its petals about midday and in the afternoon you may only find a few loose petals lying on the ground. Fresh flowers open early next morning. A few yards further on you cross a tiny stream with two stepping stones. On the left by the water's edge is a clump of **Marsh Bedstraw**, not a very common plant in Alderney.

Climb the short stretch beyond the stream and you are at the corner of a large open field, Platte Côtil, pronounced Piacerty. In the Channel Islands a 'Côtil' is a cultivated slope, usually overlooking the sea. Keep along the seaward edge of this field. At its end a short track leads towards the sea and another seat where you can rest and enjoy the view. Return inland up the

V & F stone, V side

edge of the field and you come to the 'Madonna Stone'. This slender erect stone pillar at one time was in the middle of the field above and was used by cows as a scratching post. It was moved here many years ago. In the 1960s it was noticed that a trick of the light at a particular time of day shows what looks like the outline of a woman with a shawl over her head and a child in her arms, when it is viewed from a little way off, along the gravelled road leading to the west. Hence the name. There is a seat close by.

You are nearing the end of this walk, so follow the gravel track towards the north away from the sea. You pass the end of the airport runway and in another 100yds or so reach the tarmac road again. In front of you

Another V and F stone, F side

OUT AND ABOUT IN ALDERNEY

Marais Square and the Riduna Bus about 1949/50

against the wall of the garden opposite is a white boundary stone. You will note a letter V carved on it and if you examine the other side, against the wall there is a letter F carved. This marker is made of limestone which is not found anywhere in the Channel Islands. It is one of the few remaining from the time of Queen Elizabeth I and they were brought from England and used to mark the boundaries between freehold or "Franche" land and the Crown or Lord of the Manor's land, tenanted by a peasant or "Villein" land.

When the crops were harvested, tithes due to church or Governor were set aside and counted. The land on the side facing the F paid only every tenth part of the crop whilst the Villein land owed every seventh part.

Carry on down the lane in front of you and you soon come to Marais Square at the bottom of the town. Here a drink or a snack at the Marais Hall or the Rose and Crown if the time is right, or perhaps a pasty or a pie and a can of lemonade or Coke from Le Cocq's Stores will refresh you after your walk.

Enjoy the next one!

Walk 3. Little Street to La Hêche via Quatre Vents and La Cachalière.
(About 1½ -2 miles. Allow 1½ hours).

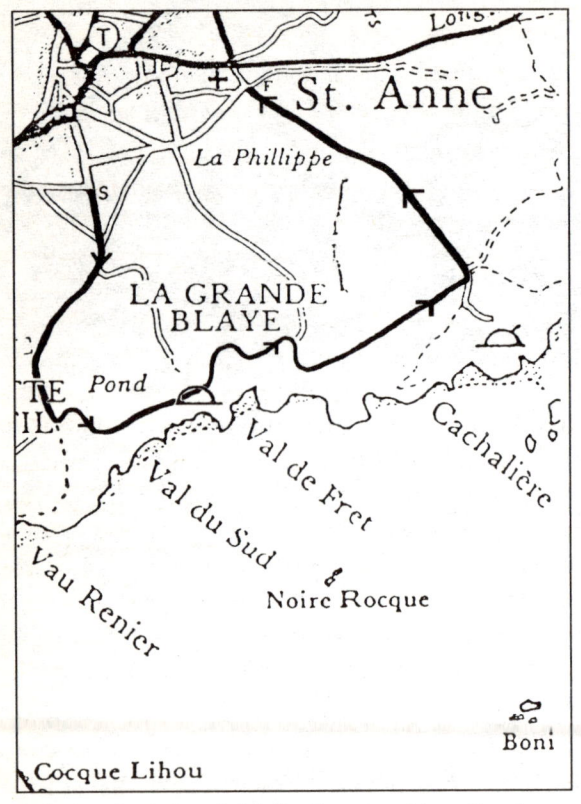

Start from the top of Little Street where the tarmac road passes the track leading towards the cliffs and Walk number 2 finished.

Follow the gravelled track across the end of the airport runway to the Madonna stone and turn left. This is still part of the 25ft wide military road which runs along most of the southern cliffs. It is however mainly used by walkers and is not readily accessible to traffic with steep gradients and encroaching vegetation. As far as possible the States keep this roadway mown to make easy walking. In about 100 yards you will see on your left on top of the stone wall a patch of pinky white **Burnet Rose**, in flower between May and July. This very prickly rose usually grows on sandy commons where it makes sitting uncomfortable. It is abundant on Herm Common and at St. Ouen's Common in Jersey, but rare here and never on the commons.

The track bears right and if you look over the wall on your left a few yards down into the Val du Saou, you will see a huge clump of the **Giant Rhubarb** (Gunnera tinctoria) with leaves 4-6ft across, above your head if you stand under them. Close to this is a large specimen of the **Twisted Willow**, Salix tortuosa. The valley takes its name from the word Saule meaning Willow and contains a lot of the common **Rusty Sallow**, Alderney's equivalent to the English Pussy or **Goat Willow**. It takes its name from these and has been corrupted over time to Val du Sud on some maps. At the bottom of this dip take the track down to your right leading through some trees and scrub to another small waterfall over a low cliff. After admiring the view, return to the path.

The wall all the way along on your left is known as the "Costière". It is the very ancient boundary wall of the Blayes, the island's open field strip system of agricultural land. Originally of stone and earth topped with furze (Gorse) to keep the cattle out of the cultivated land, it marks the boundary between the Blayes and the rough common lands on which the inhabitants were allowed to graze their animals and cut furze to fuel their ovens. These common lands were largely divided up amongst the inhabitants in 1830 and much of them is now privately owned. In modern French costière means a coastal path.

Continue along the path over a large German bunker and in front of Quatre Vents. A pre-war house which is the only dwelling on the cliffs. It has a superb outlook and was called by the German Occupiers during the war 'Million Villa' the Millionaire's House. On the cliffs in front of this are some of the island's few wild plants of the **Common Broom** and also wild **Privet**. The leaves of this are much more slender and pointed than the usual garden hedge variety. Keep a sharp eye open along this part of the track also for a **Slow-Worm** to cross your path. These legless lizards, looking like a silvery brown snake up to a foot long, are Alderney's only indigenous reptiles. Another small valley with a stream, Vau du Fret, lies just beyond the house. At one time there was a hydraulic ram here, automatically pumping water from the stream to the house. The track turns inland somewhat and a few small enclosed fields separate it from the Blayes proper. These were taken out of the Common land at a date before 1830. Above the wall, at the point where it takes a sudden sharp bend to the right is a track called La Longue Pierre. This is a "Route de Suffrance" to allow the owners of strips further from the town to reach their land and marks the turning points for the plough for the strips on either side. It got its name from the 'Pierre' or Neolithic standing stone which was once at some point along its length.

You might be lucky enough to see one of Alderney's special, but now rare nesting birds, the **Dartford Warbler**, along this stretch. A little further along on the right an indistinct track branches off to the right. This is actually on private land and leads to a German Searchlight position established above the Cachalière Pier. A granite quarry was opened here at the turn of the century and the pier was built to allow the stone to be taken out by sea. A stone crusher and a very efficient railway system for loading the crushed roadstone into ships was built. The access to the pier end was difficult, requiring skilled navigation and an expert knowledge of the tides to avoid grounding the laden vessels. It ceased to be used not long after the SS *Tyne* hit the Bonit Rock just offshore and sank in 1924

Loading stone at La Cachalière about 1920. The ship is probably the ill-fated SS Tyne

with the loss of five lives including the captain. The machinery was removed and the pier left intact, but the Germans, fearing the British would use it to invade the island, blew it up in 1942 and only one section and a few pillars now remain. The large offshore islet with its tidal causeway from the shore is L'Etac de la Quoire (pronounced like 'chair'). You might see more **Ravens** and some **Kittywakes** along this stretch.

Whichever track you take turn left away from the sea and follow the grassy roadway back towards Town. This is another Route de Suffrance called Vue de L'Etac at the seaward end, then becomes Vaindesaire (pronounced vainzaire) a word derived from the Saxon word 'wend' and signifying a strip for the plough to turn on at the end of a furrow. To the left of the track, on Le Rond But, the highest point of the island, you can see the German artillery Commander's Bunker and a survey Trig point on the skyline The track leads through a number of agricultural and contractor's buildings to La Hêche, site of one of the ancient gateways to the Blayes. Here a gatekeeper was employed and charged 2 sous for admission to the Blayes after sunset. Alderney's "New" Windmill, (erected in 1560) formerly

Cartoon by Victor Prout of Tom Lihou, Alderney's Policeman in the 1890s, by the Windmill

stood where the buildings are, the "Old" mill being formerly on a mound not far from the Telegraph Tower. There was already a windmill at this old site, a former Neolithic burial mound, by about 1200 and a mill was still shown there on maps up to the mid 19th century.

As you reach the tarmac road again the little gravelled lane on your right is the Corvée. This is named from a mediaeval custom where the inhabitants owed a service of a number of days labour each year to maintain the island roads in return for the tenancy of their land here. This custom was maintained in Sark where, until 1957, all the 'tenants' had to give some days each year, usually in November, to maintaining the roads or at least to pay someone else to do it on their behalf.

A few yards further along La Hêche, and you are at the junction of High Street, Le Val and Longis Road.

This ends the third walk.

Walk 4. La Hêche to La Tchue.
(About 2 miles. Allow 1½ hours)

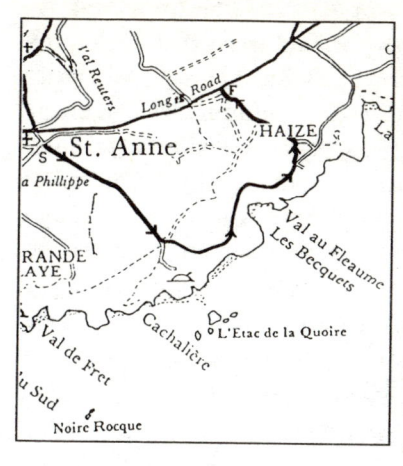

This walk starts from the cross roads at the top of High Street where you finished the last walk. Take the short street La Hêche to the junction with Le Chemin du Meunier (Miller's Road) and then follow the gravelled road between the large buildings. This soon becomes a grassy track and bears right. Follow it towards the sea until you get to a T-junction, where it meets the old military road. Turn left and at the end of the fenced field on your right, turn right towards the sea. The military road went straight on here. When you reach the top of the cliffs turn left and follow the path.

In a few yards below you on your right you will see the top of a white-painted 'Sugar-loaf' navigation cone or beacon, part way down the cliff. A faint track leads down to this but you cannot gain access to Bluestone Beach below it from the beacon. Follow the path until it turns to the left in about 50yds. You should see another very narrow track leading through the knee-high scrub more or less in front of you and bearing away towards the sea. Follow this and when it seems to split take the left-hand part. You are on the headland of Les Becquets, 'The Beaks', another spot where you might see the **Dartford Warbler**. In another 50yds this will become a more obvious track leading downwards to the cliff edge and then zig-zagging down the cliff towards the beach. Before descending, stop and admire the views. Towards the west below you is Bluestone Beach. Composed entirely of small blue-grey granite pebbles, this is a legacy from the former granite quarry just beyond the headland. Sloping down to the beach towards the far end are some smooth bare rockslides composed of Alderney sandstone. Polished smooth by the waves for centuries, their pale pink and white colour contrasts strongly with the dark pebbles of the beach. This sandstone overlays the harder rocks all the way round from the north and east coasts as far as this point. High up the cliff above these is a small colony of one of Alderney's rarest plants, the **Flax-leaved St. John's-wort**. Don't try and reach it, the ascent is quite hazardous and the return more so.

At the other end of the beach is the large offshore stack L'Etac de la Quoire, much of it grass-covered and home to many seabirds. Depending on the tide this may seem to be an offshore island or be joined to the beach by a natural causeway. If the tide is below about a quarter down and going down, you can safely gain the beach by continuing down the track and over the large smooth rocks with their criss-cross of marbled intrusion bands at the bottom to the beach. Make sure the tide does not cut you off from these if you get right onto the beach, as the track you have just descended is the only safe way back up the cliffs. There are some caves on your right. If the tide is well down you may explore round the corner beyond the causeway and you are then on the shore below Cachalière Quarry, with the remains of the pier in front of you.

The beach shelves sharply into deep water and it is possible to dive from the rocks. If you decide to swim, make sure the tide does not take you out as it is quite strong here. The beach is rarely used except by a few hardy souls who want an all-over tan. The simplest and safest approach is by sea, provided your boatman knows the waters well.

If you have simply stopped at the top of the final descent, the view behind you to the east includes the French coast and the Hanging Rocks, sticking out at an angle from the Alderney cliffs in the distance. Return to the wider path at the top of the

Bluestone Bay

cliffs. The stone bank is again on your left, the enclosed fields behind it were again taken from the Common lands at an unknown date, before the 1830 shareout and you follow it round a semicircular bay. A sharp corner in the wall on your left there marks the point where the ancient open field system once more comes to the Costière at the side of the military road. This rises and falls with the slopes of the small steep-sided valley and at the bottom of the next dip there is a short track to your right leading down to one of the old cattle troughs collecting water from the small stream here. The States usually keep the pathway leading down to this cut, although it is extremely rare for cattle to be watered here now. The views from here are quite splendid with an excellent view of the Hanging Rocks. Return to the old road and in another 150 yards you reach a tarmac road, just above the gateway to the island's rubbish dump, known as the 'Impôt'. Turn left along this and in about 350yds you will reach the Longis Road opposite the Catholic Cemetery. The two sets of gate pillars you have just passed between mark the boundaries of one of the German Camps, *Lager Borkhum*. This was a camp

The Priest's vault in the Catholic Cemetery

principally for technicians, sometimes German, but often from occupied Europe, who had skills needed by the OT (Organisation Todt) which supplied labour for the German factories and defence works. At first they were paid, brought here for a few months for a particular job and then repatriated, later it became one of the slave camps. After the island was relieved by British Forces on 16th May 1945 it was occupied by them and renamed 'Minerva Camp'. You may have noticed the concrete bases of some of the huts on the right as you passed along. On the left near the newer cattle building are the remains of two other old brick kilns. The concrete building on your left just before you reached the main road, with a radio mast above it, was the German Underground Hospital. Now used as the Alderney Civil Defence Emergency HQ and also as the HQ of the Royal Alderney Junior Militia. It has a direct telephone link to the MOD and radio transmitters capable of reaching London.

Whilst you are at this point you may like to make a quick tour of the Catholic Cemetery. It was established in the 1850s, during the period when the Breakwater and Forts were built, for the benefit of the Catholic immigrant workers. The largest tomb towards the top is the burial place of several of Alderney's Catholic Priests and some of the Nuns from the Convent, which was formerly in the building now the Island Hall.

OUT AND ABOUT IN ALDERNEY

German Naval funeral in the field next to St. Michel, February 1942

Turn uphill towards town and on the next corner a few yards away is the Cimitière St. Michel, the 'Stranger's Cemetery'. This was established in 1802 at a time when there was a large garrison of British Troops. Disease caused many deaths and the parish churchyard was too full. This land already belonged to the church, being the probable site of the Chapel of St. Michel, one of the several 'Frairies' which existed in Alderney until Henry VIII's dissolution of the monasteries in the 1530s. It was therefore consecrated for the burial of those who were not born in Alderney. It is no longer used, but in the spring is beautified by the island's only colony of **Cowslips**. Against the far wall, opposite the gateway, leans a large stone with its legend in German. This was erected in the field the other side of the wall which the Germans took as a cemetery for those of their troops who died here and 11 bodies from the sinking of two German ships by British MTBs. It was erected, after the island was relieved, by the remaining German POWs to "Our Dead Comrades!". The gospel quote is actually from St. John 14:19 and not 14:20.

Follow the main road on up the hill and you are soon back at your starting point.

Walk 5. La Tchue to The Nunnery via Essex Hill.
(About a mile. Allow up to an hour to admire the views).

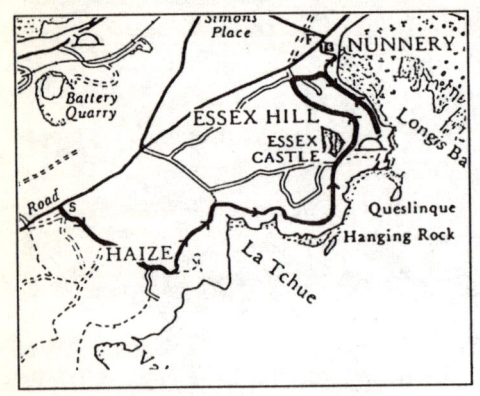

Start at the junction opposite the Catholic Cemetery in Longis Road at the point where Walk 4 came out, and return along the side road to the gate of the Impôt.

Just before this on the left is a sign indicating 'Cliff path'. Follow this. The track winds round the top of the quarry where the rubbish is burnt, now once again screened by bracken and gorse after a large heath fire here in the late 1980s. As the track turns left and starts to run downhill, the bay below the quarry is called La Tchue which means 'backside'. I have not been able to discover if this name was given before the rubbish dump was established here in Victorian times, or after. The appearance of this narrow inlet could also have been likened to that part of the anatomy and might possibly have been the original name from long before the rubbish was pushed over the nearby cliff. The swift currents at the foot of the cliff rapidly disposed of everything from domestic waste to old cars and lorries which provided a good home for **Conger Eels**.

Recently a great deal more attention has been paid to sorting and burning and only the ashes and soil are pushed over. Metal waste, including old cars and domestic equipment is burnt, crushed and taken away by boat for scrap about once a year.

Beyond the bottom of the dip another track leads off to the left. Keep right along the cliff amongst the heather and gorse.

In early spring keep a lookout for the tiny blue and white star-like flowers of the **Sand Crocus** which are all along the track here and in bare patches either side. In autumn, look out for the tiny mauvy-blue flowers of the **Autumn Squill**, like a miniature Hyacinth. Earlier their small flat circles of bright green curved leaves with a groove along the upper side can be seen all along the ground up to the top of the hill. In summer the hillside is brilliant with **Gorse, Sheep's-bit** and **Ox-eye Daisies**. Below on the more gently sloping cliffs you will see the brilliant pinky-mauve flowers of the **Kaffir Fig** with their fleshy dark green Mesembryanthemum type leaves and a patch of bright red **Lampranthus**, a smaller Mesemb. These both originate from South Africa and their seeds were probably brought to the island with the baggage of the Army Units which had served there before their posting to Alderney.

As you gain the top of Essex Hill, in late August and September look for the 4in dull green spikes of the **Autumn Lady's Tresses** in the shorter turf. This little orchid has small white flowers arranged up the stem in a spiral. Nearby, the old

Coastguard Lookout during the war

railings with some cast iron gateposts are all that remains of the Coastguard Lookout point, built in 1906. The house, with its hexagonal lookout from which the Race and most of the south coast could be seen was also used by the Germans as a lookout, but was demolished after the war. All that remains now are the railings, the red-tiled floor of the lookout and a tank which may have been the cellar of the house or simply a collecting point for storage of the rainwater from the roof. It is now home to a large clump of **Greater Reedmace**, more commonly thought of as **Bulrushes**, and a few **Water Lilies**. The fine submerged weed with little white star-like flowers is a recent invader, the **New Zealand Water Crassula**. This small, rapid spreading, plant is now causing considerable problems in the UK where it is clogging canals and inland waters.

Near the tank you will note some large iron hoops set in concrete. These are the anchor points for the first radio telegraph mast erected here in 1905. The small hut where the telegraph was operated has been restored recently as an animal isolation hospital or quarantine area for small animals.

Erika inscription

Keep over to the cliff top. Here there are the remains of several German installations. If you have sharp eyes you may notice the name "Erika" cut into the cement on the top of a low wall. Perhaps this was the name of the soldier's wife or girl friend, but it was also the code name for a sophisticated German tracking system of the period. Maybe there was one here at the time??

Within a few feet of this wall there is a patch of the very rare **Land Quillwort**, a most unusual fern, most of whose close relatives live in mud at the bottom of ponds. All you will see above ground, if you look very carefully in the spring is a circle of curved linear leaves 2-3in across, very like the more frequent **Autumn Squill** which is also found nearby. The remainder is below ground in a small bulbous base. The spores are produced at the base of each leaf and, when ripe, escape up the leaf to the surface. The plant requires growing conditions in small sandy hollows, flooded in winter and drying out in summer. How it got here and survives is a mystery.

Not much further on another, rather overgrown, track leads to the Hanging Rocks, sandstone pillars leaning out from the cliff face. There is another small German gun position just above them. These were somewhat higher before the war, but the Germans blew the tops off the two largest to clear a field of fire for one of their larger guns.

There are several legends about these rocks which are also known locally as 'Madame Robilliard's Nose'.

The Hanging Rocks

1. Betsey Robilliard was a nosy old woman who pried into the affairs of a *sorcier*, or wizard, living on Platte Saline. He put a spell on her which caused her nose to grow to an enormous size. It was removed by an exorcist for the price of three pigs. The sorcier managed to obtain it and set it up as a landmark and a warning to other nosy people.

2. The best known legend concerns the Guernsey 'Donkeys', as the inhabitants of that island are called by the people of Jersey and Alderney. They were jealous of the Alderney folk and went to the Devil for help in making fools of them. The Devil tied a rope to a great rock sticking up vertically on the side of Essex Hill, flew back to L'Ancresse Common and gave the other end to the Guernsey folk, telling them that if they pulled all night, in the morning Alderney would be theirs. They all heaved and pulled with great shouting and pulled so hard that they bent the rock over at an angle, but Alderney did not move and the laugh was on them.

3. Finally, the angle at which they hang is attributed to divine intervention when Alderney was threatened by Norse Pirates in the 8th or 9th century. The Priest prayed for a miracle to drive them away and, as they sailed into the harbour at

Longis Bay, the rocks leaned out of the cliff over them and they were so scared that they turned and fled.

Return to the track and take it towards Fort Essex. The cream painted Fort was built in 1869 as a barracks and garrison hospital. The original entrance to the fort is between the two small square guardhouses in front of you. The present entrance to the left, below the German lookout, was made during or just after the war.

For the construction of the barracks, the keep or donjon and much of the walls of Essex Castle, which was then known as 'Les Murs de Haut', (built between 1546 and 1560, to guard the original harbour in Longis Bay) were demolished. All that remains now of the castle, on the far side from your present position, is the eastern and part of the northern walls and bastion, with the 'Pepperpot' lookout added about 1810.

Fort Essex is privately owned and converted into a number of large flats. It was sold off at auction by the War Office in 1930 at the same time as several of the smaller forts and fetched £30.

There was a large Anti-aircraft battery established on top of the hill here during the war and many of the emplacements are still to be seen, near another Trig point, to the left of the Fort.

Descend the tarmac road. Across the bay is Raz Island with its Victorian Fort and Causeway. Down below you, just above the sea, you will note a number of much older fortifications

Longis Bay and Raz Island with French coast beyond

dating back to the Napoleonic Wars. On the right, just beyond the small house you can see at the foot of the hill overlooking the bay is the 'Frying Pan' Battery, so-called from its shape. Several other gun emplacements, with the magazine behind them line the top of the low cliff to the left of this. In front of these from about half tide down you can see the remains of the old jetty as a line of large stones at right angles to the low cliff. This was rebuilt in 1660 on the orders of Charles II on the site of an earlier jetty.

The slate-roofed buildings behind the battery were the officers quarters, the other barracks being long gone. At the bottom of the hill are two pillars, recently built, but similar in style and position to those shown here on a print of 1830. Beside them is the Essex Manor Restaurant. In Napoleonic times the home farm and barn of the Governor's estate. It was then turned into barracks, later became an inn with a bad reputation as a smuggler's haunt. In Victorian times the troops used it until they were banned because of its bad reputation.

A print of "Ruins of Essex Castle" about 1830

For much of the time since the last war it has been a restaurant and bar, formerly known as 'The Old Barn'. Here for most of the day in the season, except on a Sunday, you can get a snack or a full meal, outdoors if the weather is fine. There is also a shop selling the work of local craftsmen and artists.

Take the track in front of the restaurant and at the end of the hedge either continue on to look at the old gun emplacements, returning to the same point, or cross the field to your left. This brings you to two stepping stones across the stream flowing down the Val Fontaine to the island's sewerage treatment plant with its well tended garden and the car park at "The Nunnery"

Here you will find public toilets and several seats overlooking the sea. A number of local fishermen keep their boats here and pull them up the slip when bad weather is feared. The German gun emplacement was built across the line of the ancient cobbled 'Vraic Road', a roadway built for the farmers' carts to get down to the beach to gather seaweed (or vraic) to fertilise their fields. If the tide has pulled the sand back, a small section of this can still be seen on the beach just in front of the seats.

The Nunnery has its origins in a Roman Fort built about AD 375. Bits of Roman brickwork and roof tiles are often to be found on the beach after a storm clears the sand back. Archaeologists, at the end of the last century

The Nunnery

and in the 1920s and 30s, uncovered the remains of other Roman buildings near here, a number of Roman graves and the remains of a burnt out Roman boat. Items from these finds are on display in the Alderney Museum. A flattened bronze bucket from about 500 BC was also found. Carefully restored by the Portsmouth City Museum, this 10in high bucket is now on display in the Guernsey Museum

This was the island's main defensive position, overlooking the original harbour until Les Murs de Haut were built in Elizabethan times. It was then known as Les Murs en Bas, (the 'Lower Walls' or the Walls Below). It had a round bastion at each corner and the gateway was in the wall facing the car park area. Some time in the 1600s the eastern wall collapsed onto the beach where it remains to this day.

Renewed fears of invasion by the French towards the end of the 18th century caused the Governor to have the wall rebuilt in its present position. A new covered gateway was constructed facing the road and the present houses inside were built as a barracks in 1793. It acquired its name about this time when the English army garrison thought they were living like Nuns so far from the town and the girls. The two nearby inns being apparently little consolation for the loss of feminine company. Today it is owned by the States and the barracks has been divided into houses bought on long leases.

Remains of Essex Castle, 1989

The interior of the Nunnery too was modified by the Germans and outside there is another large gun emplacement covering the length of the beach. This point also marks the start of their vast, but not completed anti-tank wall. Today this makes a fine south-facing shelter for people using the beach. It reflects the heat and helps to cut off the wind.

Longis Common in front of you was probably the site of the earliest settlement in Alderney. At many points, both across and above it, evidence of Neolithic, Bronze Age, Iron Age, Roman and later occupation by man has been found. If you have time, walk up the road opposite the gate for a few dozen yards. On the left you will see a sign "Iron Age Site". Follow the track onto the golf course and in 50yds or so you come to a rounded flat area with a few rocks showing in the grass. When the Golf course was being constructed in 1968, in a field known for centuries as Les Huguettes and called the "Potter's field" in the 1830s, a quantity of pieces of pottery was turned up by a bulldozer. This was recognised by the Museum Curator as coming from late Bronze Age or early Iron Age pots. The green was resited and over the next two years, the Curators, Ken and Peggy Wilson excavated what turned out to be a pottery

Les Porciaux in 1906

manufacturing place dating to about 490 BC. From the pieces of pottery found some 36 more or less complete pots were reconstructed. Several are on show in the museum, with other bronze, bone and stone items found there. There must have been quite a large settlement nearby to justify such a pottery.

At the time of the Common Lands division in 1830 many ancient burials were unearthed by people cultivating the land for the first time for many centuries, or building their homes on it. Flint, stone and bronze tools and weapons were also found. Much was destroyed in ignorance, but some records have survived. Across the other side of the common near the site of the house now known as Sharp's Farm, in 1832 a collection of about 200 bronze tools, implements and weapons, many of them broken, was found just beneath the surface, together with a 12lb lump of copper. This was suggestive of the presence of a Bronze Age foundry nearby. These items are all in the Guernsey Museum where many of them are on permanent display.

For centuries two large Neolithic Dolmens known as Les Porciaux stood up at the far end of the common where the road goes uphill. They got their name from the resemblance, from a distance, of the standing stones around them to a herd of pigs grazing. The dolmens were excavated by the Lukis family from Guernsey in the 1840s-50s, but the Germans removed the standing stones during the war and turned one of the burial

Bronze Bucket c. 500 BC from near the Nunnery

Iron Age pots, c. 490 BC from Les Huguettes site

chambers into a gun emplacement. Little can be seen now except the flat capstones amongst the bracken.

In recent years several bronze axe heads dating from about 500 BC have been found on or around Longis Beach. Many flint tools have been found in the submerged peat beds in the bay and two wooden spears dating from about 4,000 BC have been found. One of these and some of the tools are on display in the Alderney Museum.

If you have no transport arranged, you must now walk back to Town either up Bluestone Hill to the left, or take the Route des Mielles in front of you to Braye Bay. In the season the bus will pick you up here by the Nunnery gateway, at about 25 minutes past the hours of 10,11,12,2,3 and 4 on its return journey from the beaches.

OUT AND ABOUT IN ALDERNEY

Part of the "Alderney Hoard" of Bronze Age Implements found on Longis Common in 1832

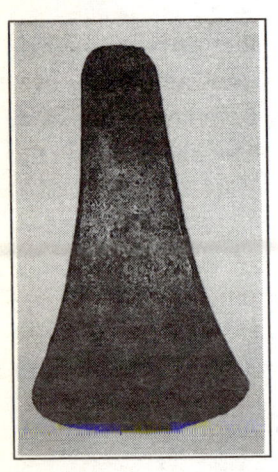

Bronze Age Axe head, c. 2,000 BC found at L'Emauve

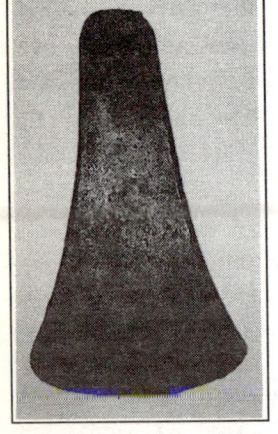

Lead pan weight, 1lb troy. Early 15th century. Used for weighing bread at that time. Found near Essex Castle in 1928

3. The West coast

These two walks overlap for part of their length. In following either, if the tide is right, walk along the causeway out to Fort Clonque for some fine views of the west coast. The offshore bird sanctuary island of Burhou with its attendant reefs, the swift tidal passage of the Swinge, the Gannet Colonies on Les Etacs and Ortac, and the Casquets Lighthouse are in sight from almost the entire length of both walks. If the weather is clear you will also see Guernsey about 20 miles away.

This area has been the scene of many wrecks over the centuries, the remains of two can still be seen at low tide.

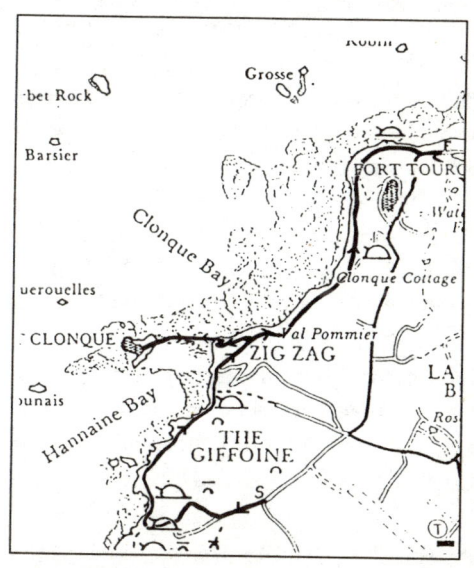

Walk 6.
The Giffoine to Platte Saline.
(*About 2½ miles, nearly all downhill. Allow about 2 hours if you go out to the Fort as well*)

This walk starts at the same point as Walk 2, at the end of the tarmac road leading from the junction of Le Grand Val and the road from Fort Tourgis.

Follow the gravelled road to the first fork and take the right hand part again. In about 100yds, the bare part of the roadway crosses a little bridge over an old German tunnel and turns left. Go straight on here along the grassy track. You reach the top of the cliffs above a large German bunker with Hannaine Bay below you.

A small colony of **Puffins** nest in the cliffs here. When the sea is calm you may well see them swimming underwater over the large sandy patch amongst the rocks. The Casquets, Ortac and Burhou are in front of you once again.

Turn to the right and all along the path, in midsummer, keep a lookout amongst others, for the **Glanville Fritillary** butterfly. Easily recognised by the dark brown net pattern on its golden/orange wings and quite common in Alderney, it is only found in the Channel Islands and in a very small area of the Isle of Wight. Keep to the undulating path along the cliff top and, after crossing a broad dry valley follow the path up the steep northern side of the valley towards the sea. At the top you will find a seat to rest on with a good view of Fort Clonque and the offshore reefs and islets.

You are now a few yards from the apex of one of the bends of the Zig-Zag. Follow it downhill and there are other seats from which to stop and admire the view. Just above the last seat before you get to the bottom, close to the cliff edge you will see a square WD marker stone. This one marks the boundary of the strip of land all round the coast, 100ft from high water mark, reserved by the Crown when the Common lands were shared out in 1830. This was intended to allow for later fortification works, and military access to watchpoints, but meanwhile the inhabitants were allowed to dry their vraic (seaweed) on the strip. Not a very practical proposition now after more than a century and a half of cliff erosion at this point.

Descend further onto the flat part. Here you can trace the outline of the walls of the 17th century Clonque Barracks in the short turf by the car parking area. Troops were stationed here then to man a small

Fort Clonque from the Zig-Zag

gun battery on the cliff in front of them to guard the sea passage through the Swinge. There was a lookout hut up on the hillside behind you. Its remains can still be seen, just above the track where the small square of trees are situated.

In a few more yards take the track to the left and descend to the causeway out to Clonque Island. This was built about 1850 to improve access over the natural tidal causeway to the islet. It was strengthened by the Germans in 1944. As you approach the fort, on the right notice the earthen bank above some large boulders. At the top of this you will see a thick layer of well worn, sea-rounded pebbles set in the soil. This is part of a 'raised beach', a remnant of one of the ice ages about 150,000 years ago when the sea level was much higher than today. The fort was completed in 1855. It mounted ten guns and had a complement of 59 men. Sold off by the War Department with several other forts in 1930, it went for £ 27 at auction.

Since 1965 it has been owned by the Landmark Trust who paid £ 19,000 for it. It is now used as a holiday home sleeping twelve, for their employees. It can also be hired by the week for parties of up to 12 if it is not otherwise booked. A local craftsman, Arthur Markell spent nearly twenty years here bringing the central part of the fort, which had been somewhat adapted by the Germans, into a state as near as possible to that of Victorian times. This included replacing the drawbridge across the dry moat. In the late 1960s the natural bridge joining the main part of the fort to No. 3 battery was washed away in a great storm. The battery now stands isolated on a rock pinnacle. At low tide you can walk right round the outside of the islet.

If you do, in midsummer you will see the daisy-like flowers of **Golden Samphire** along the base of the walls in several places. Keep a sharp eye out in August for the pinky-blue-grey flowers of the **Rock Sea Lavender** on their slender wire-like stalks above rosettes of small spoon-shaped leaves. Please do not be tempted to pick these, they are quite rare. Also around the edges and in the car parking area you will see plenty of the greeny-yellow flowers of **Rock Samphire** with its finely cut grey-green leaves. This is a member of the Parsley family and quite unrelated to the Golden Samphire. It is common on most of our rocky shores. Its leaves can be used to make a pickle with a strong bite to it. Also in some quantity you will note the white flowers or greenish seed heads of the **Sea Carrot**. Common all around the island close to the sea, its feathery grey-green leaves are easy to recognise. Further inland the similar looking **Wild Carrot** is more likely to be found.

If it is not occupied, the fort may be inspected by arrangement with the Warden whose telephone number will be found on the plaque at the landward end of the causeway.

Clonque Islet in former times was the scene of revelry on the first Sunday in Lent, remnant of a pagan fertility rite to celebrate the return of Spring, known as Les **Brandons**.

The young people of Alderney, as in most other communities elsewhere, assembled to feast and dance at the time of the spring plantings, in order to ensure the fertility of the crops.

This Bacchanalia was held here, where they all repaired in their best clothes, with musical instruments, to picnic and dance, play kissing games and make other entertainments. In the evening a huge bonfire was lit, after which they all danced back to the town bearing torches of rush (or *gluie*), or made from twisted straw. They ran through the streets waving these to the great danger of the thatched roofs of the houses. In the early 1700s the Governor of Alderney tried to have it banned because of the danger to the houses. By about 1800 this pagan custom had become a time for dancing, feasting, singing and exchanging kisses. At nightfall the Brandons, (torches), were lit and the youngsters went in procession to the town. Despite this attempt to ban it, it continued well into Victorian times, in the late 19th century. It died out completely early in the 20th century, although the garrisons at various times have held sports days ending in feasting, dancing and fireworks, or to celebrate Royal visits.

This custom was revived in spirit in August 1971, with a torchlight procession through Town becoming part of the Alderney Week celebrations. Now it forms the climax to the whole week of festivities.

Return along the causeway to the military road and keep to the left at the junction. In 100yds or so you come to a narrow valley on the right. This is Vau Pommier (meaning Apple Tree Valley). One wonders if there was not a cider orchard here at some time in the distant past. It is now overgrown and impassable. The stream comes from springs higher up, where, when the old barracks were established, there was a washing place and water source for the soldiers. All along here large old bushes of **Ivy** are thickly topped with spherical bunches of bright yellow flowers in October. The buzzing of late flying bees collecting nectar from them on a warm day is almost deafening. In spring you may see the bees carefully scraping the waxy surfaces of the leaves to enable them to make their honeycombs.

Below you to the left you can just see the end of one of the ancient cobbled vraic roads on the beach. This was a good spot for collecting seaweed for the fields, great banks of it collect here after every storm. Go a few yards further through the little avenue of trees and go down the grassy track to the beach. At the bottom on the left is the 'Blue Bridge', a lovely Victorian culvert of blue granite and brick, built

"Blue Bridge" at Vau Pommier

to carry the road over the stream. A larger part of the cobbled vraic road still exists just here, and if you go down onto the beach, below the level of the present bridge is the square stone culvert of a much older outlet for the stream.

Go back to the track above and continue on. Tiny fields, now much overgrown, were cut for hay before the last war. You come to an old fisherman's cottage where you can now buy goat's milk, yoghurt and eggs. Here, one night in 1922, the owner's dog woke the family up barking. They heard shouting out in the Swinge and could see the masthead light of a steamer close in. The owner lit a lantern and slipped down onto the beach. He was able to guide the ship's boat, with the whole crew of 11 men and a woman on board, into a gully so that they could walk ashore. He took them to the cottage for the night. In the morning the 750 ton collier *Emily Eveson* was to be seen, wedged into a gully between higher rocks. Her boiler and propeller, stempost and hatch-comings can still be seen there at low tide. Her cargo of anthracite kept local families busy collecting it for a long time after.

Remains of the SS Emily Eveson in Clonque Bay

Along this part of the walk you will nearly always see at least one **Kestrel** hovering and swooping for the prey it has spotted. Along the shore line, **Oyster Catchers**, several species of **Gull** and the occasional **Heron** fishing may be seen. During the spring and autumn migrations a number of smaller waders appear for a week or two.

Nearer the shore is a grey chair-shaped rock, one of the last to be covered as the tide comes in. This is known locally as the Chaise à la Moine the Monk's or Devil's Chair. It still bears witness to the struggle of a monk with the devil who tied him to the rock to drown, but he survived due to divine

HM Queen Elizabeth II with President Jon Kay-Mouat,
outside the Island Hall, 24th May 1989.

Miss Alderney Float 1991,
L-R, Victoria Saint, Sally McAllister (Miss Alderney),
Lorna Neill (runner up).

Gannets on The Garden Rocks

Puffin

Burnet Rose

Giant Rhubarb

Dartford Warbler

Sand Crocus

Autumn Squill

Lady's Tresses Orchid

Glanville Fritillary Butterfly

Alderney Sea Lavender

Peacock Butterfly

Tormentil

Bell Heather

Slender St. John's-wort

The Alderney Geranium

Pyramidal Orchid

Viper's Buglos

Orange Bird's-foot

The Garden Rocks in mist

The Casquets at sunset

Small Hare's-ear

Bastard Toad-flax

Bermuda Grass

Hairy Onion

Enchanter's Nightshade

Cowslips

Field Geranium

Old Man's Beard

Blond Hedgehog

Black Rabbit

Burnet Moth on Ragwort

Kaffir Fig (Yellow variety)

Alderney Week torchlight procession 1994

Fishing and pleasure boats in Braye Harbour

intervention, an alternative version of the legend to the one which follows.

The Monk's Chair was also reputedly the place to which a monk from La Moinerie on the eastern end of the island in the sixth century walked every morning and sat meditating. A group of islanders engaged in 'wrecking' early one winter's day were driving a cow along the shore with a lantern tied between her horns to lure a ship onto the rocks when the monk came upon them. When they found themselves discovered they tied him to the rock and left him to drown on the incoming tide. His ghost is supposed to be seen in the chair whenever a wreck is about to occur on the coast.

The house beyond the cottage was built after the last war. Up the track to the right is a German searchlight post to enable them to illuminate the Swinge. Take the left fork in the track here and in a few yards on your right, about 5yds back from the track you will see another square WD marker stone. "Boundary 100ft to the Sea". This has the same function as the previous one but it would still be possible to spread seaweed to dry here, if the brambles and bracken were cleared.

The huge grey bulk of Fort Tourgis is now on the hill in front of you. Also completed in 1855, built on the site of an ancient watchtower, it mounted 33 guns and the barracks accommodated 336 men. Last used by the army in the 1950s it then became flats for immigrant Italian farm workers, but has been derelict for many years. Plans are currently afoot for it to be developed into a complex which will restore the magnificent structure and bring long-term revenue to the island.

Two more old vraic roads along the track here give access to the beach. Depending on the weather and the state of the tide you may see a huge area of flat rocks, with many interesting pools amongst them between the low cliff and the sea. **Sea Hares, Sea Cucumbers**, the **Sea Mouse** and an unusual bright green marine worm called **Eulalia** can be found here, together with many other more common sea creatures and plants. The Swinge may be calm at slack water or have a strong tide running at about 8 knots in one direction or the other. In rough weather, towards high tide enormous waves sweep through the passage and crash on the shore, or burst on the emergent parts of the reef. In sunlight after a storm they offer a spectacular sight of sea-green water and white foam. There have been many wrecks in the Swinge and on Burhou over the centuries. The little house on Burhou was originally built in the 18th century as a refuge for fishermen and shipwrecked mariners. Used by the Germans one day in 1942 for target practice for one of their guns, later restored after the wartime damage, it can now be rented as a self catering holiday place, sleeping six, by application to the Harbour Master' office. Be warned, you have to take your own water and all other supplies with you!! The Harbour Master now supplies users with a two-way radio to contact help in case of emergency.

A week after a successful raid on the Casquets when several Germans were captured and taken to England, there was a British commando raid on Burhou, known as 'Operation Branford', led by Capt. Colin Ogden Smith on the night of 7/8th September 1942, but they found the house destroyed and the island deserted.

The small car park below the fort walls is sited between a dismal looking German concrete bunker, now fortunately almost covered with **Kaffir Fig**, with pink or sometimes yellow flowers, which housed a 10cm gun to cover the beach areas in case of allied landings and the much more elegant Victorian caponnière with its musket slits. From here at low tide you get a much nearer view of the square black engine of the MV *Armas* just off the right-hand end of Burhou.

Another 2 or 300yds, with the walls of one of Fort Tourgis' 8-gun batteries looming over you with another German searchlight position at its eastern end brings you to the main

MV Armas *perched on the Nannels Reef, 26th November 1963*

road at Platte Saline. The square concrete block with a hole in it was the hingepost of a German gate to prevent access to the coast road and another 10cm gun emplacement covered the length of Platte Saline beach from this end.

You are now at the end of this walk and can make your way back to Town, seen above the hill in front of you, dominated by the roof of the church tower and the ugly concrete German water tower, by way of Le Petit Val ahead, with a seat at the bottom for the weary. If you turn left, the second turning you reach past the Tennis Club, Le Vallée, at the T-junction, or the narrow Butes Lane going steeply up from just above the same junction, both take you up to Town.

OUT AND ABOUT IN ALDERNEY

Platte Saline in rough weather

Alderney and Gourey Lifeboats exercising off Platte Saline with Sea King Helicopter

Walk 7. The Zig-Zag to Platte Saline.
(About 1½ miles, all downhill.
Allow about 2 hours if you go out to the Fort as well)

This can also be covered on a bicycle, but you must not ride down (or up) the Zig-Zag part. This is a shorter version of the previous walk, taking in the whole of the Zig-Zag path.

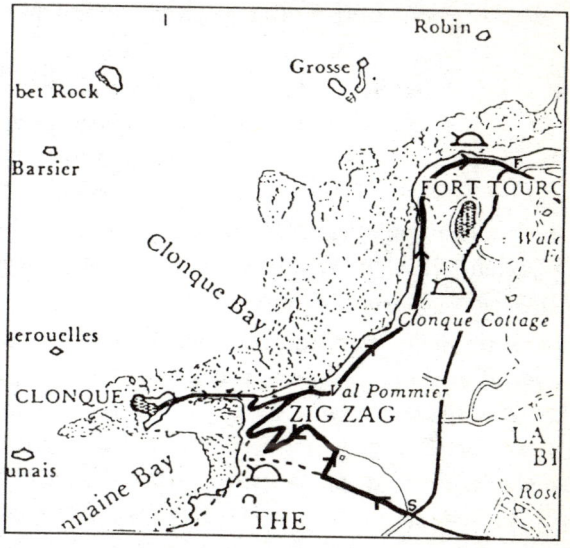

Start from the junction of the road from Fort Tourgis and Le Grand Val. There is a signpost here indicating the Zig-Zag. Follow the track and take the first branch on the right. To your right here is a ruined building with four, different style, WD marker stones at the boundaries of the plot. Inside is a pump over a deep Victorian well. There are large collecting tanks built underground here and the water originally flowed by gravity feed from these to Fort Tourgis, just out of sight below the horizon to the north. Much of the nearby concrete work is German. The pump was driven by an engine at first, but after the war this was replaced by an electric motor. It is no longer used.

Keep to the track as it bears left. You will shortly see two small square concrete posts in the path. These bear the initials ER and a number. They are two of hundreds placed round the island after the war to mark the boundaries between plots of the open field system. The Germans had removed most of the pre-war markers and the British Government employed three land surveyors in succession, two of whom died on the job, over a period of about 10 years to re-establish the ownership of the land.

In the 1960s the fields on La Petite Blaye, the 'Little Blaye' from here towards the north and east were the centre of a very active flower growing industry. Daffodils and Iris were the main crop, pickers were flown over from Lincolnshire to help gather them and in one year more than 2 million blooms were sent to Covent Garden Market. The trade died when the regular boat services were withdrawn.

On your right just past the markers the slight depression marks the top of the Vau Pommier referred to in the previous walk. There is a spectacular view of the west coast from here. At the next corner Fort Clonque is straight in front of you, perhaps the best view of the fort is from here, with the causeway stretching out from the land, barely above the water at high tide. Hannaine Bay lies to the left, its sandy bottom offering a safe anchorage for yachts waiting for the tide in the Swinge to run in their favour so that they may reach Braye Harbour in safety. Clonque Bay lies to the right and the whole length of the sandstone reef from the Casquets to the Grosse Rock lies before you.

As you descend the Zig-Zag, several well placed seats allow you to rest and take in the view. Along the bank on the left of the first downward slope you might find, in June or July, the small, bright, 5-petalled dark yellow flowers of another of Alderney's rare plants, **Slender St. John's-wort**, this one is however locally common in Britain. In mid-late August the

The hut on Burhou about 1930

Bell-heather and **Ling** here is often swarming with **Silver Y Moths**, a day-flying brown moth about 1 in. across, with a pale 'Y' shaped mark on each of its upper wings. Amongst the heather are many dark green cushions of **Tormentil**, covered for several months of the year with 4-petalled pale yellow flowers. The **Gorse** here too forms small, rabbit-nibbled cushions of pale greeny-grey foliage with its bright yellow strongly scented pea flowers.

The path from the previous walk joins the Zig-Zag at the apex of the next bend, and from here on your walk covers the same ground back to Platte Saline. Look out for **Peacock Butterflies** and note the many plants of **Bird's-foot Trefoil** along this route, with its yellow pea flowers, often flushed with red.

4. The North coast

The North coast, (facing England about 60 miles away) is in general flat and only about 30ft above sea level. There are many off-shore rocks and reefs, some only emerging below half-tide level. The whole area is dominated by the remaining half-mile length of the Breakwater (originally almost a mile long) and the series of Victorian Forts built to defend it. If the sea is calm, walk along the length of the Breakwater for a fine view of the Bay and the Town.

The next walks can also be easily accomplished by cyclists. The first two start and finish in Town.

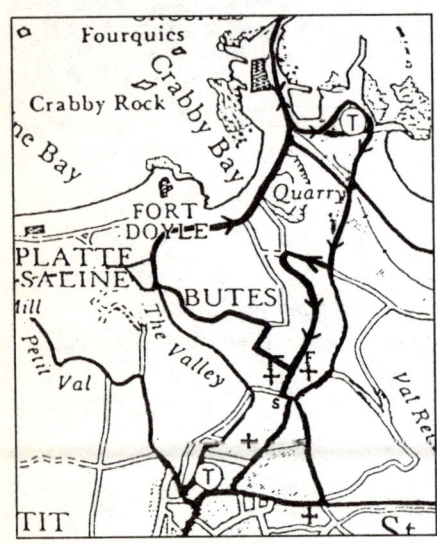

Walk 8. The Butes to Platte Saline and the Harbour, returning to the starting point.

(About 2 miles including the Breakwater. Allow 1½ hours).

At the bottom of Victoria Street, the Methodist Chapel, built in 1851 is on your left. Take the road in front of it past the Belle Vue Hotel to the Butes car park. Keep on the road to the left of the old Militia Arsenal and Gun shed, now the Alderney Public Works Depôt. At the corner, on your left notice a concrete plinth, with a curious half round tapered groove in it, on top of the wall. This was erected in 1891 for the Lloyd's signalman to place his telescope on, which trained it directly on the semaphore on the Casquets Lighthouse, until the house behind the wall was built in recent years. He could thus get news of ships as they passed the light and send it on to London by the electric telegraph. There was another semaphore mast erected on Butes at this time, with a hut for the signalman. The station was closed about 10 years later.

To the right of this plinth is the site of the former Grand Hotel. The Butes Shed on the other side of the road was formerly the Militia Gunshed. It was turned into a military hospital about 1880. The new Youth Centre just beyond was opened by the Queen in 1989. Turn left by this and follow the narrow winding lane down to the bottom. Cross the road and continue towards the harbour. On your right the new house behind the high wall is built on the site of the former RC Presbytery, demolished by the Germans during the war. Next to this the archway was formerly the entrance to the RC Church built in 1847. The Germans used this as a potato and swede store and it was in such bad condition in 1945 that a new church was built in Braye Road a few years later, to replace it. The cobbled former vraic road leading down onto Platte Saline just in front of you also leads to Fort Doyle. Go down this track. The Fort was built in 1854, with 4 guns, on the site of another 4-gun battery built in 1816. German gun emplacements either side of it covered Platte Saline and Crabby Bays. It is now used as the HQ of the Alderney Boxing Club.

Retrace your steps a few yards and go through the cutting. This was originally made to allow the narrow gauge railway needed to carry stone from the nearby quarry to build forts Doyle, Platte Saline, Tourgis and Clonque. The nurses home for the hospital is just above it. There was formerly a village here of 2-storied workers houses, built when the Breakwater and Forts were under construction, but demolished by the Germans. Alderney's Mignot Memorial Hospital, opened in 1959 is up the short lane across the road from here and the new

St. John's Ambulance Station, built by public subscription in 1991 is just below it.

The railway ran along just above the beaches, at the time in front of the Platte Saline Battery on land now long eroded away. It connected to the standard gauge railway at the harbour. Shortly after emerging from the cutting, on your left is a short, low, grey wall. Look down over the top. It is actually the entrance to a tunnel which before the war carried the cobbled vraic road down to Crabby beach under the road way. Further on on the right is York Hill Quarry. A **Wild Pear** tree grows on the corner nearest to you. The narrow lane alongside goes back up to Butes. The quarry was the first to be opened for stone to build the Breakwater in 1847. It now houses the island's Power Station and the water in the quarry is used to cool the generator's engines. In spring and summer it is home to a small colony of **Terns**.

In May and June a small area of the grass immediately above the beach is the only site in the island of the **Bithynian Vetch**, a pinky-mauve and white, pea-like plant, with much larger flowers and leaves than most vetches.

Next on your left is the large shed which now houses diving equipment and the tanks for starting the conservation of objects recovered from the exiting project of Alderney's Elizabethan warship wreck. If the door is open, do stop and have a look at some of the objects, videos and photographs on display inside. Donations towards preservation costs of the items recovered are welcomed. The building was originally built as stables for the horses used to tow the wagons loaded with stone along the narrow gauge railway and on top of the Breakwater.

Behind this is the more recent building which houses the Channel Jumper factory and shop. Here you may buy thick Alderney's, a type of heavy sweater like a Guernsey, with the lion of Alderney's Arms knitted into the chest. Lighter garments are also available and many of these can be embroidered with your name or other logos whilst you wait. They also sell ice-cream and offer a Bureau de Change service.

Another vraic road, washed away many years ago stood here. You may sometimes see a section of the cobbles uncovered by the sand on the beach below the factory.

You are now at the harbour. On your right the corrugated roofed building behind the oil tanks is Alderney's earlier power station, in use until the present one was built in 1952. This was started in the period just before the war to supply electricity for the huge stone crusher which formerly stood on the bare triangular area next to it. It is now a petrol station and car hire depôt. The tanks hold heating oil for retail sale. The crusher, built in 1905, had been steam operated previously and was finally demolished in the 1960s. The buildings behind were, from the 1840s, the Engine sheds and workshops for the mineral railway. They now house a marine engineer's and a metal worker's premises. Railway lines still lead into them and the whole of this area carries remnants of railway tracks as well as the line still in use by the Alderney Railway Society, which runs out to Mannez Quarry.

In front of you some seats overlook the "New Harbour" otherwise known as "Little Crabby Harbour". Built in 1847 to shelter the barges and vessels engaged in building the breakwater. Just to the right of the seats are the bases of the two lime kilns built here at the same time to burn the lime used in mortar for the forts. On the left is the glacis of Fort Grosnez, the first fort to be built between 1851-3, to protect the landward end of the Breakwater. It housed 112 men and mounted 28 guns. Since the last British Garrison was withdrawn in 1929/30 and the Royal Alderney Artillery Militia was disbanded, it has been used by the men and machinery engaged in maintaining the Breakwater, a continuous and costly business.

The Inner Harbour and Fort Grosnez

If the weather and sea be calm, take the road between the Fort and the Harbour and walk the half-mile length of what was intended to be the western arm of a "Harbour of Refuge", a thinly disguised term for a Naval Base. The eastern arm, in the final plans, was to extend out from Château à L'Etoc enclosing about 150 acres of sea, but was barely even started before the project was abandoned, after well over a million pounds had been spent on the first arm. Fine views of the Town and Harbour can be got from here, and good fishing from the end if that is your interest. Walk out along the upper deck and then return along the lower level. Queen Victoria paid three visits to Alderney during its construction to observe progress. When first completed in 1864 it was almost a mile long. Winter storms continually swept parts of it away and after about 1870 it was shortened to its present length and the army of several thousand workmen left the island, only a hundred or two remaining on quarrying and maintenance work.

At the far end you may well see the underwater part, about 20 feet down at low tide, extending out beyond you at a slight angle to the remainder. Wave patterns often mark this line clearly and in rough weather a line of breakers form over the sunken part. It has caused the destruction of a number of vessels over the years which have not gone far enough out to clear the end.

Returning from the Breakwater, just past the old coal yard and Blacksmith's Shop, go down the slope to the inner harbour and walk round it. Local fishermen now principally use it, but it dries out at low tide so their boats are often moored in the bay. Yachts can come in for fuel and water at Mainbrayce in the far

The Annual Blessing of the Fishing Fleet, 1991

corner. You pass the bases of the old lime kilns, now used as stores. The steps beside them lead you up to the Braye Chippy, open all day in the season for snacks, drinks, ice cream and meals. Sit outside on the terrace when the weather is fine.

The slope leads on up to the Harbour Office. here you can get information about the day's weather and a selection of tourist leaflets. When the harbour was built a nine gun battery extended from the harbour office to the Old Harbour, built on the site of a smaller c.1740 battery, to defend the harbour roads. The plaque on the wall by the steps to the Alderney Sailing Club premises, commemorates the evacuation of the island on 23rd June 1940. It was dedicated by the island clergy exactly 50 years later and unveiled by the Mayor of Weymouth, the port where they landed on that fateful day. Many of those who left Alderney that day were present at the ceremony, including Mrs Phyllis Forsyth, daughter of Rev. Le Brun, Alderney's Vicar from 1886 to 1929. She was just a few weeks short of her 100th birthday, and has recently celebrated her 104th.

The Sapper's Slipway lies just before you, built by army engineers in the late 1950s for the Sailing Club dinghies. Next to that a new floating pontoon and ramp is provided for the benefit of yachtsmen. The Commercial Quay was built in 1897 after several years of bitter controversy between rival parties who were for and against the scheme. As a result the head of Alderney's administration, Judge J.A. Le Cocq, who had been against the project resigned. The "Jetty", as it was then called, proved an immediate benefit to the island. Goods could be loaded and unloaded without the need for lightering, passengers could come ashore without having to climb down ladders to waiting boats or onto the beach when the tide went out. Alderney's economy, in the doldrums since the end of the construction works, at that time was becoming almost totally dependent on the export of stone from the quarries and on tourists. Existing harbour facilities were convenient for neither.

Exports of stone rose dramatically within months and boatloads of tourists came by steamer excursions from several south coast ports, the other islands and from France. Carriages, and later taxis and buses met every incoming ship and large numbers of islanders thronged the quay on "Boat days" when the *SS Courier*, Alderney's regular supply boat from Guernsey arrived on its three or four times a week run, (twice a week in winter).

A stone crusher was built on the land close by in 1905 to make roadstone for export to England. Quarrying provided the main employment in the island until the evacuation in 1940, when over one third of all the working men were employed in it. It was not restarted after the war, except on a small scale for Breakwater maintenance.

Today excursions are far less frequent and there is almost no chance of islanders getting off by boat for a day out in Guernsey, Jersey or Cherbourg. Most people fly here, the 12 minute journey from Jersey or Guernsey, or the 45 minute flight from Southampton being infinitely preferable to many than the 2 -7 hours from Guernsey or 8 -16 hours from England the smaller steamers used to take depending on the weather. Despite this, in the season Braye Bay is generally thronged with yachts.

Continuing round the harbour area you have the large shed used by Alderney Shipping for cargo, the Arrivals Hall with

Customs checks and toilet facilities for sea passengers, the Harbour showers and laundry for the visiting yachtsmen and the R.N.L.I. Station. This was also built by public subscription and was opened in 1987. Alderney's new larger lifeboat *The Earl and Countess Mountbatten of Burma*, prototype of the new fast-afloat boats, is moored across the quay in the harbour. She came on station in March 1994, ten years after the station was first set up. She will be replaced soon by *Roy Barker 1*, the fourth vessel of the same class to be launched. This has been built from a legacy of £ 6.5M to the R.N.L.I. in 1993 from Jerseyman Roy Barker. The R.N.L.I. shop sells a range of goods, some produced locally and the funds generated all help to keep our lifeboat at sea and maintain the building. Plaques listing the rescues in which the Alderney Lifeboats have participated will be found on the outside walls of the Station.

A row of seats overlook the bay here. Most days you will see a line of **Shags** drying their wings on the rocks in front of you. More rarely a **Cormorant** might be there as well. The "Old Harbour" was built by the Governor of Alderney, in 1736, to replace the original harbour at Longis, from the proceeds of privateering and smuggling. The lower level, known as the Douglas Quay, was added in 1840. It began to silt up soon after the Breakwater was built and could not deal with vessels of any size, drying almost completely at low tide. Public toilets are sited just beyond, down at the beach level. The hotels, pub and houses along Braye Street are all based on the warehouses built between 1736 and 1753 to store the goods brought into the "New Pier" as it was then called. John Wesley spent a night in a room above what is now the Diver's Inn, when he was caught here in a storm in 1787. He preached a sermon on the beach next morning before departing.

There is ample choice of restaurants and accommodation here, an off-licence, bicycle and moped hire, ice cream for sale. another petrol station and car hire, a body-repair shop and

Jean's Stores where most provisions can be bought. Jean's Stores is also open on Wednesday afternoons and Sunday mornings when most of Alderney's shops are closed.

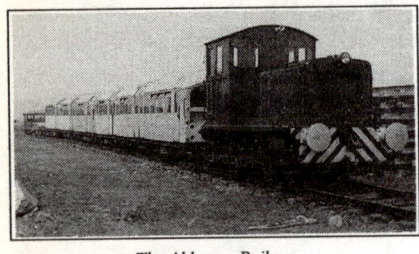

The Alderney Railway

At the end of the street is one of the Victorian public pumps and cattle troughs, installed to supply Braye Village and across the road Braye Station. The Alderney Railway Society run trains from here out to Mannez Quarry about 2 miles away. Times are posted on the station building. The railway is the only working line in the Channel Islands, is entirely run by volunteer enthusiasts and provides an attraction for young and old. In the season it is usually open on Wednesday, Saturday and Sunday afternoons. During Alderney Week and at other busy times daily services run. On Sundays refreshments are available at the Quarry end. The other of Alderney's two **Wild Pear** bushes is alongside the track near the Tea Hut.

The present stock consists of two London Underground carriages pulled by the diesel locomotive *Elizabeth*; the diesel locomotive *Molly 2*, which was used for many years on the Breakwater and several small petrol driven Wickham Railcars. Our steam engine *J.T. Daly* with its line of open canvas-topped trucks is alas no longer with us. Restored, it now runs on a private line in Jersey.

Cross the lines and carry on up the hill. The pink washed bungalow on the left with an old cannon on the wall is called 'Peacehaven'. Built by the German's as quarters for their naval officers, it was the place where the German Military Commander signed the surrender papers in 1945. The two tables on which the surrender was signed can now be seen, one

The Breakwater in a storm

in the Museum and the other in the States' Chamber. Each bears a small brass plaque commemorating the event.

Opposite is a short flight of steps and one of the harbour navigation lights. At night, ships lining this beacon up with the light on the head of the Old Harbour, can safely miss the sunken part of the breakwater when entering port. On the level ground here, formerly stood another parochial school, erected about 1850 for the children of the immigrant workers and used as a chapel on Sundays. During the day, ships entering harbour can line the white painted navigation cone on the old pier up with the Church tower. Just past the line of trees, take the unmade road which leads you back up the hill to Butes and the start of your walk. At the top of the track the Children's Playground and public toilets are on the left, and on the right, with a magnificent view of the harbour and much of the northern side of the island, a row of seats offer another opportunity to sit, rest and gaze.

Walk 9. The Butes to the Harbour and the Arsenal, returning to the starting point
(About 2½ - 3 miles including the Breakwater. Allow 2 hours)

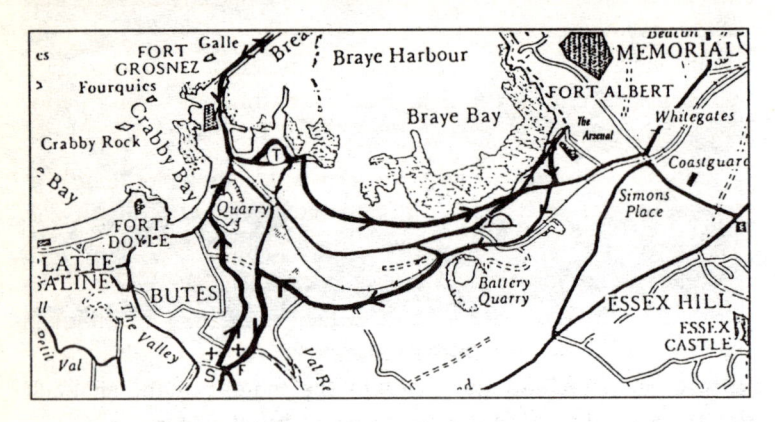

This walk also starts on Butes, but this time keep on the grassy side of the Cricket Club and Butes Centre and take the downhill path on the left hand side of the green. Above one of the smaller quarries on the right of this track, in May or June you should find a large clump of the rare pink/blue Tassel Hyacinth. You emerge at Crabby Bay with the Power station on your right.

Follow the route of Walk 8 to the harbour, along the Breakwater and back to Braye Street. Here you may either walk along the beach towards the Arsenal at the far end, or, at high tide, follow line of the old road known as Le Banquage along the top of the dunes from the end of the street, along Braye Common to the same point. If you take the beach route, look out along the base of the dunes at the end nearer the harbour for the small, dark green, prickly bushes of **Prickly Saltwort**. Also along here you may see the pale green finger like leaves of **Sea Rocket** bearing pale mauve flowers in August/September. The taller grey-leaved plants with bright yellow flowers and long, thin, curved seed pods are the **Yellow Horned Poppy**.

Just above here at the top of the dunes, is a large patch of **Wild Clematis** otherwise known as Virgin's Bower or Old Man's Beard. Its creamy yellow, star-shaped flowers are at their best at the end of August or in early September and the seeds with their long hairy beards then persist for much of the winter. This plant is common in England but only grows in three or four spots on Alderney.

Several German Bunkers can be found along the length of the beach and on the rocks in the middle at low tide you will see the boilers and ribs of two ships just beyond them and inshore on the left the remains of a smaller vessel lies on its side. The larger two are the wrecks of the *SS Burton* and MV *Henny Fricke*. *Burton* was wrecked in January 1911 after loading granite chippings at the jetty. She struck the Grois Reef off Château à L'Etoc after leaving harbour and was towed back to Braye but broke in two here and sank. *Henny Fricke* was a 300 ton German supply vessel which sank here in a storm in 1943 right on top of the *Burton*. Attempts to tow her off failed and she was left to rot. The smaller wreck inshore of these was a German Harbour Guard vessel *VP 703*. She struck the rocks and sank whilst attempting to tow the much larger 515 ton *Xaver Dorsch* off the beach. She had broken her moorings and run ashore in a great storm in April 1943 whilst loaded with slave workers who were being taken back to France. Many were drowned in the hold, but the ship was towed off a few days later and was sunk by the RAF off the French coast a year later in April 1944.

In the last century and up to about 1920 there was another steam driven stone crusher sited on the first part of the common, just beyond the first sandy lane leading down onto the beach. Buried some way under this is probably the remains of the cobbled road which once gave access to the cellars of the warehouses. From about 1868 the Telegraph Office was also just here.

Across the common beyond the present road, there is gradually developing a new "village" between the common and Newtown. Newtown was built in the 1840s to house the Breakwater workers, Le Banquage housing scheme is built on States' Land leased for a nominal sum to island born people to build their own homes. Much of the site was formerly a huge heap of quarry spoil from the Victorian quarry behind, removed to give access to stone for the breakwater and forts. As you can see, this is still being cleared to give access to additional land for new houses. In earlier times after the "New Pier" was built there was a large Gun Battery, Elizabeth Battery, built on the elevated ground where the quarry now is, to defend the bay, with another, St Anne's Battery, with 9 guns, below it on the common. Other batteries at the harbour and on Roselle point on the far side of the bay completed the defences here.

At the end of the common, opposite the harbour entrance, another line of seats gives you an opportunity to rest your legs, admire the view and watch the comings and goings in the harbour. Here is also the site of another of the vraic roads giving access to the beach. This one has been rebuilt after coastal erosion destroyed the earlier one. In a NE gale the sea frequently washes seaweed and shingle across the road and the low cliff has had to be reinforced several times. Lower Road and the original track now meet at this point. Lower Road, running from the top of the rise by the railway crossing at Whitegates back to Braye Station was renamed Rue de Beaumont in 1992 in honour of the twinning of Alderney with Beaumont Hague, where the French nuclear reprocessing plant is sited on the hill just across the Race. The new name has not met with popular acceptance however and is rarely used.

Follow the track across the rest of the common to the gateway of the Arsenal. In June and July keep your eyes open for the many lovely triangular pink heads of the **Pyramidal**

Orchid which grows in this area. The impressive bulk of Mount Hale Battery on the small hill formerly called Mont Allai on your right only mounted one gun to protect the Arsenal and some mortars which covered Braye Bay. The Arsenal and stores depôt had a drawbridge at each of the two entrances, a musketry step all along the wall overlooking the beach, and the covered gallery with musket slits leading up to Alderney's largest fort and the last to be built, Fort Albert.

This was built between 1856-59 on Mont Touraille, where a watchtower had stood since Elizabethan times. Originally called Fort Touraille it was renamed in his honour after the Prince Consort died in 1861.

Retrace your steps along the tarmac road and cross the Lower Road onto the grassy track up to the railway line. Either side of this in midsummer notice the small bushy clumps of the **Rough Star Thistle**. The heads below the flower are covered in white star-shaped prickles. It has grown at this spot for well over a century but has not spread much and has never been found elsewhere in Alderney. Walk along the railway track, (but watch out for the occasional very slow-moving train in the summer). You pass through a cutting with concrete bays used to load the blocks of stone from Battery Quarry just behind them, into the railway trucks. An elaborate overhead hoist system was built here to allow the blocks to be lifted up from the quarry bottom. This was eventually about 150 feet deep. Tall anchor tripods locally called blunds were built just above the shore and at the top of the Rochers above the quarry with strong cables stretched between them. A system of pulleys then enabled the stone blocks weighing 2 or 3 tons, loaded into iron scoops to be pulled up by horses from below and tipped into the waiting trucks.

The quarry is now the island's principal reservoir and, when full holds over 40 million gallons. Formerly fed only by run-off from the hill above, by rainfall and springs, it had a back-up pipe allowing water to be brought from the reserve reservoir at Corblets which holds up to about 14 million gallons. In the 1986 drought this reserve was virtually emptied for the first time is twenty years and the level in Battery Quarry got dangerously low. In 1993 a new main was laid across the island to the pumping station near Fort Tourgis. Here the island's principal stream, which, up until about 1920, had powered the Watermill, supplied more water than could be dealt with by the station pumping directly into the supply via the storage tanks at the Allée ès Fées. The excess ran to the pond which had existed for centuries on Platte Saline. From the 1970s when the needs of the increasing population for water, especially with the installation of modern appliances, rose considerably, this had gradually turned into a marshy area, almost completely dry in summer.

Most of this excess can now be pumped directly back to the Battery Quarry and when this is full on to Corblets Quarry.

Along the railway track here look for the small mauve, Groundsel like flowers of the **Blue Fleabane**. A few yards further on, the other side of the road crossing is one of the sites of another of Alderney's special plants, the **Alderney Geranium**. Differing slightly from the common **Dove's-foot Cranesbill**, it has recently been given full status as a separate species. The plant is generally about 12-18in high and has 1/2 in. pink flowers borne in pairs on thin bent stalks. On the hill above you are the island's TV and Radio relay masts.

Follow the road along past the petrol pumps, builder's merchant and a line of houses. Opposite these a former German encampment housed a canteen, turned after the war into the Penguin Club which was eventually burnt down and buildings which became a car Silencer Factory for several years. Here also the Germans had a small prison where they put workers who had misbehaved in some way. The two semi-basement cells with the guardroom above are still there beside the railway track.

You are now in the 1850s "Newtown". Birdcage Walk on the right seems to have got its name in Victorian times when Irish Ladies-of-the-Town sat in the windows of the houses here and plied their trade. Part of The Harbour Lights Hotel on the left was formerly the site of Alderney's Gasworks, opened in about 1860 and in use until the evacuation in 1940. The main bar of the hotel with its curved wall is built where one of the gasholders stood. On the left immediately beyond is the bottom of the 'Water Lanes', properly called the Fontaine David. One of the old well heads formerly supplying the Newtown is just round the corner of the buildings. Opposite is the water pumping station and treatment hut.

Several narrow lanes of Victorian workers houses lie on the right, running towards the sea. On the main road Mother Friday's

Some of Alderney's Guernsey Cattle behind Fort Albert

House got its name from the habit of the mother of a large family to sit on the doorstep on Fridays and collect the pay packets as her family came home from work in the quarries and on the Breakwater.

Just beyond the last lane is Alderney's Public School, opened in 1969 when it moved from the 1790 building in Town, now the Museum. It caters for all ages from 4-15 and in 1992 had 15 teachers and 163 pupils. The swimming pool was given to the school in 1975, and by 1990 the P.T.A. had raised sufficient funds to enable the changing rooms to be built.

OUT AND ABOUT IN ALDERNEY

Val des Portes portico

Children here can take the GCSE courses but the opportunity is given to those who pass the 11+ exams to go to the Grammar Schools in Guernsey.

At the end of the road turn left and walk up the hill back to town. Half way up, a small public garden offers seating for those feeling in need of a rest. The large house, Val des Portes, just above it was built about 1800 from the profits of privateering by the Robilliard family. The portico over the door has nautical embellishments which presumably commemorate this association. For many years this has been the residence of the Kay-Mouat family. Jon Kay-Mouat was President of the States of Alderney from 1977-93. His father was a Jurat of the Alderney Court from 1938-53. One might assume from the

The Arsenal and Mount Hale Battery from Fort Albert

name of the house, at the bottom of Le Val, that there was a gateway to the Town here at some distant time.

The new Catholic Church opposite was completed in 1973 after 20 years in building. The bells were installed in 1980 with another added in 1988. There is a parish room below where jumble sales and many other functions are held.

On the corner above the house the rather derelict cream-washed triangular building was a pub called the Birmingham Arms in 1880. It later served as the Convent School until that moved to the Island Hall about 1890. In 1920 it became St. Anne's Club. Formed for returning ex-servicemen and other islanders, you can still see the remains of the words 'Billiard Room' over the lower doorway. The club disbanded many years ago, the St. Anne's trust was dissolved about 1992 and the property is for sale, still complete with the billiard table.

Turn right here and you are back at your starting point, the bottom of Victoria Street.

Walk 10. Whitegates to Fort Albert, Saye Bay and Château à L'Etoc, returning to the starting point.

(Only about a mile, but allow an hour or more to explore).

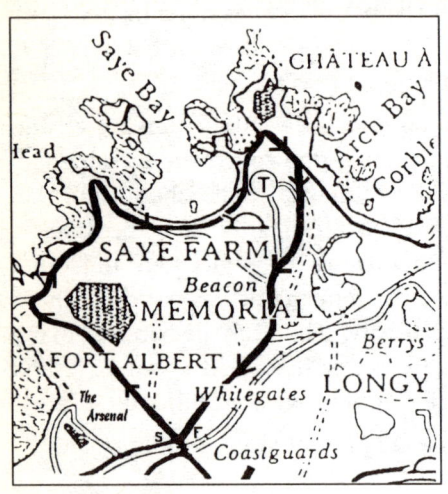

You can use your car or the bus to get to Whitegates to start this walk. Whitegates got its name from the level crossing gates which were here in Victorian times. The houses were built as married quarters for the families of the garrison with 4 officer's houses at Simon's Place on the rise just across the tracks, now overlooking the golf course.

The island's football pitch with its recently built clubhouse is on your left. Leave your car nearby and walk up the gravelled road to the fort. In Victorian times a golf course was laid out on the slopes of the Glacis on your right. When you come level with the first dry moat of the fort, stones in the roadway mark the former position of a rolling drawbridge with a small guard post alongside. The old Fives court for the garrison is just below to the left. It now houses the island's squash court. Another rolling drawbridge was sited by the upper dry moat and on the left here, at the top of the covered ramp leading down to the Arsenal two field guns were kept to cover any attempt to assault the Arsenal. Above you the great height of the Fort wall has musket slits all along to aid the defence of the Arsenal complex if needed. Continue on up the track. The bank on your right in early summer is ablaze with the pink and blue flowers of **Viper's Buglos**, uncommon in

England these days. The track to the left leads down to Roselle Point with the remains of its former gun battery and on the extremity the housing for the "Electric Light Battery" a searchlight position established in 1905 to illuminate the harbour entrance if attacked. There are some Great War additions here as well as the several more recent German bunkers. There have been a number of wrecks on this point over the years.

The interior of the Fort is not open to inspection but you can cross the bridge where another rolling drawbridge was originally positioned and see through the gates the mess left after the army blew up the barrack blocks there in the 1970s. At the moment the fort is used by the States Agriculture team as a store, the Clay Pigeon Club shoot here on Sunday mornings and one of the German bunkers was converted in 1993 to house the relay stereo transmitter for Island FM, the Guernsey based commercial radio station. Studio facilities will soon be provided for Alderney to make its own broadcasts within the island for an hour or two in the evening when required, or for use in a civil emergency.

Seats along the path here give yet another opportunity to stop and admire the views of Town, harbour and the offshore islands in the Swinge. About 90% of the houses in the island can be seen from here. In the opposite direction most of the eastern end of the island from Fort Essex round to the Lighthouse is visible.

Along the path, below you lie a mixture of old and more recent fortifications. Several of the bunkers are accessible and worth a

Dolerite vein near Roselle Point

brief visit. Climb up the bank behind you to the top of the outer walls of the fort and look down into the deep dry moat. Elegant musketry caponiers flank each angle of the unusual five-sided fort which is fitted so neatly onto the contours of the original hilltop as to be almost invisible from the sea.

Continue on downhill. The hillside and the headland below you are a honeycomb of bunkers, trenches and underground passages which formed a German infantry strongpoint. More seats will be found here. The large 10cm gun emplacement on Bibette Head is well worth a visit. Just here too there is an interesting geological formation. Bibette Head, unlike most of the surface rocks on this side of the island, is composed of granite with a fault of dolerite across it. This shows as a black band about a yard wide with peculiar rounded patches. At the base of the cliffs a rare formation known as orbicular diorite occurs. This shows as concentric circles of various coloured rock. There is a fine specimen in the Museum.

Retrace your steps from the headland to the gravelled road. Alderney's safest swimming beach, the almost circular Saye Bay (pronounced Soy) is in front of you. The clean almost white sandy beach with the Camp Site behind the dunes, gives no hint of the horrors of the slave camp established here during the war in the quiet tranquillity of this lovely spot. The green painted house at the end, a former farm now run as a guest house, was originally built as the office for the engineer superintending the building of the eastern arm of the breakwater.

Walk along the beach or the edge of the camp site, just behind the dunes. There is a camp shop, open in the season, public toilets and a telephone here. At the far end of the camp site there is a tunnel leading to Arch Bay, another favourite swimming spot. The tunnel was originally a bridge built to carry the railway line, used to take stone for the building of Château à L'Etoc and the proposed eastern arm of the harbour, over the vraic road giving access to the beach for carts to pick up the seaweed. Go through the tunnel and climb back up the short grassy bank to the road.

During the war the camp site was another slave camp, *Lager Norderney*, with about 1,500 prisoners. Mainly inhabited by French, Poles, Spaniards and Algerians, with Jewish prisoners kept in a separate inner camp, it had a bad reputation for the harsh treatment they received.

Château à L'Etoc, now on your right, commanded both the harbour entrance and the bays on its eastern side. It mounted 23 guns in 7 batteries and had barracks for 128 men. The old barrack blocks are now turned into flats, many occupied by States' workers.

Return along the roadway past the Camp site and farmhouse. The pole on the left with a triangle on top is a navigation beacon. Lined up at sea with a similar beacon offshore of the Château it enables shipping to clear the sunken end of the Breakwater safely. Just beyond it is the Hammond Memorial.

The gardens here are maintained by the owners of the nurseries at Longis Bay, at their own expense. It was built by the Hammond family to commemorate the slave workers of many

Hammond Memorial service

nations who died in Alderney during the war. Plaques in their various languages are fixed to the walls, and the ashes of the three members of the Hammond family who conceived the idea and built it are now buried here. The site overlooks the area of Longis Common to the south where more than 300 of these workers were formerly buried. An annual ceremony takes place in May at about the time the island was liberated. For many years the Russian Ambassador in London or the Military Attaché have come to remember their dead and lay a wreath.

Hammond Memorial after service

French survivors of the camps, few of whom are now left alive, have also come each year. The remembrance service is shared by the clergy or representatives in Alderney of each of the religions whose adherents are commemorated here. The British Legion and the Royal Alderney Junior Militia provide a guard of honour and a trumpeter to sound the Last Post. A considerable portion of the population attend in most years.

Splendid views of Longis Bay, the Common with its pond and reed bed, and Essex Hill are to be had from here. This area was probably the site of the earliest settlement on Alderney. Many of the principal archaeological finds have been made around its periphery in the last 150 years. In the last five years further survey work and small excavations have uncovered further evidence of stone age, bronze age, iron age, Roman and mediaeval occupation. Island tradition calls the area Mondainville, a name which will not be found on maps.

A few hundred yards further on you are back at the starting point.

5. The East coast

This is the flat NE and SE coast of the island including the Lighthouse, several Victorian forts and many offshore islets and reefs. It can easily be accomplished in one walk.
It is also the scene of many more wrecks over the years. The remains of one can still be seen at low tide.

Walk 11. Château à L'Etoc to the Nunnery.
(Approximately 2½ miles. Allow up to 2½ -3 hours)

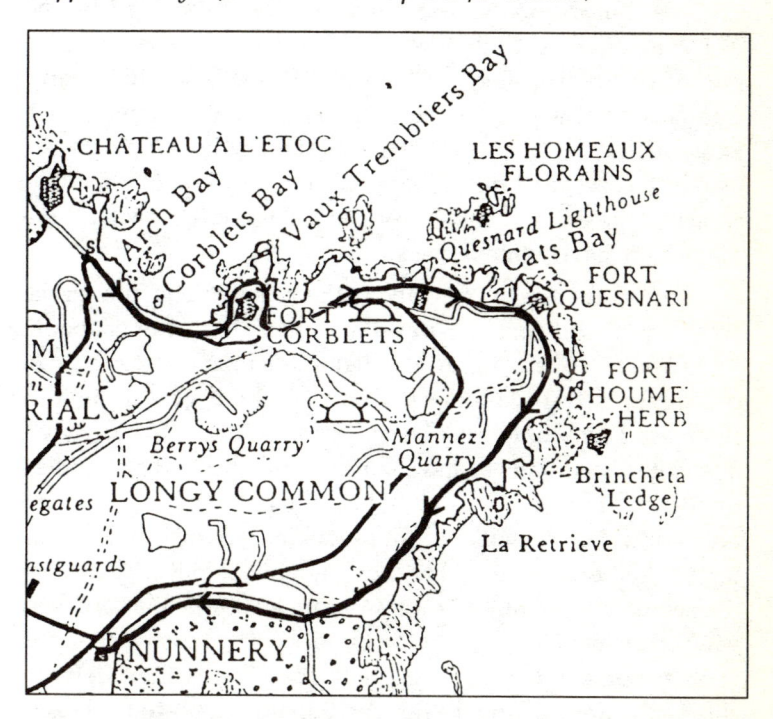

This route can easily be followed on a bicycle, or take the bus out to the Camp Site. At the start Arch Bay lies a few feet below you down the bank with the old railway bridge on the left. Just offshore from Château à L'Etoc you should see the white buoy marking the site of Alderney's Elizabethan Wreck on Les Grois Ledge. You might even see divers working there at slack water in calm weather in summer

If the tide is low you can go down here and walk along the beach. Above about half tide it is cut off from Corblets Bay which lies more or less at right angles.

At this corner a German bunker is set in the low rock face above you on the opposite side of the road. Access can be gained up the iron rungs set into the rock face. Just beyond is Corblets Quarry now a water reservoir and also used by the Alderney Angling Club. The partly submerged hut housed a pump to supply water to Château à L'Etoc when the quarry was closed. It is one of the best places in the island to see **Dragonflies**. Here also the **Hoary Stock** whose flowers are usually mauve, and quite common in other parts of Alderney, clings to the cliffs in some profusion. For some reason all the plants here have white flowers.

Keep on the rough track above the beach. Frequently in the season you will find the travelling snack bar "Roundabout" parked here. Ice cream, drinks, hamburgers and hot dogs can be bought if you are hungry. Almost in front of it a flight of steps lead down to the beach. This is one of Alderney's favourite swimming and surfing beaches. 3-4ft rollers frequently come in in a straight line along the full length of the beach and the occasional yacht moors in the sandy bay. At the top of the beach a broad band of shingle has piled up against the sea defence wall, built a few years ago after the road was washed away in a storm. At the far end of the beach facing you another gun emplacement covers the beach area. To its left is a slip road, another former vraic road giving access to the beach. Behind it rises the bulk of Fort Corblets.

Built in 1855 at the same time as the others along this part of the coast it mounted 13 guns and accommodated about 60 officers and men. This is now a large and expensive private home, currently for sale, with an asking price of over £ 1M. It was sold by the States to one of its members in the 1950s for £350.

Take the path through the bracken just above the bunker and walk round the base of the fort. There is a profusion of wild flowers along here, including more specimens of the pink **Kaffir Fig** so frequently found near the forts. This clump is in a sheltered position and usually has some flowers on it for about 8 months of the year. Just below you is the remains of the Alderney fishing boat *Dunlin* wrecked here in 1990. The crew of two swam ashore safely. The next bay round is Vau Trembliers. Until the huge Mannez Quarry, across the road, was excavated it was at the end of a small valley. It possibly got its name from the Aspens which could have grown here then, or perhaps from the motion of the water on the corrugated rocks which form the floor of the bay.

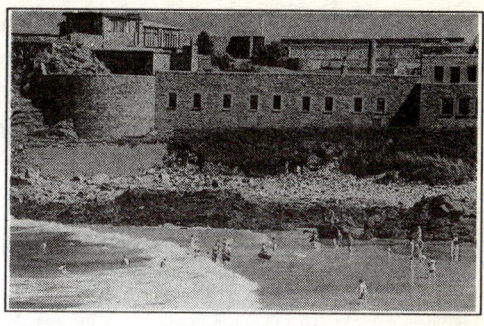

Fort Corblets and Bay

Look out to sea at the large emergent rock just off the next headland. You will note that the top of the rock has the appearance of a Lion's head. This curious feature looks the same from the other side if seen from a boat. The low cliff around the bay has a narrow flat area

Lion Rock

where eight tiny quarry workers houses were built in the 1850s. If you take the path across this bit you will see the traces of the bottom of their walls and a small cobbled yard. The field just before these, on your right, bears some of the remnants of a market garden scheme which the owner of the fort operated in the 1950s and 60s, a beautiful crop of **Wild Daffodils**, the ones about which the poet Wordsworth was so lyrical. These however were planted and are not part of Alderney's natural flora.

Across the road is the end of the railway line going into the Quarry. High above it is the most dominant of the Occupation fortifications, the *Marine-peilstand* or fire control tower. Its three floors each controlled one of the three main gun batteries around the island

The Odeon

and a huge rangefinder was situated on the roof. It formerly stood further back from the cliff edge. Post-war quarrying to repair the Breakwater has partly removed the cliff in front of it so that it now stands balanced precariously on the edge. A complete gun emplacement nearby fell down into the quarry a few years ago. Beneath the cliff, opening onto the quarry floor, is a semicircular German tunnel several hundred yards long and about 10ft in diameter

Known locally as the Odeon from its resemblance to a pre-war chain of UK cinemas, the fire control tower has further floors below ground level. The interior structure is now dangerous and you should not attempt to explore it. Behind this overlooking both sides of the island is a vast complex of gun emplacements and bunkers, many now partly buried beneath encroaching vegetation.

At the far end of the quarry is a large shallow lake, Mannez Pond. Alderney's only area of really open fresh water filled by rainfall and occasionally drying up in drought years. Here you will find many things to interest the naturalist.

All of Alderney's seven species of **Dragonfly** and **Damselfly** breed here. The pond is home to **Common Frogs** and a few of the now very rare **Jersey Agile Frog**, both imported at some time in the past and neither indigenous. A pair of **Coots** and a pair of **Moorhens** usually breed here. You may well see a **Grey Heron** looking for fish and rarely a **Purple Heron** drops in for a few days rest in passage in the autumn. Many small **Warblers** can be seen in the reed and rush beds around the pond. The large clump of "rushes" across the other side are the only colony of the **Lesser Bulrush** in the Channel Islands. In spring look for the white buttercup-like flowers of the **Water Crowfoot** along the margins and in midsummer the pink emergent flower spikes of the **Amphibious Bistort** fill the middle of the lake. Floating around the edges you may see the fairy cushions of the **Water Fern** a subtropical plant which seems to like it here. In May/June in a grassy area which is flooded most winters, you might find the curious 3in green spikes of another fern, the **Adder's-tongue Fern**, looking for all the world like miniature **Arums** (which last are often known as **Lords-and-Ladies** or **Jack-in-the-Pulpit**).

In the short rabbit-cropped turf this side of the pond and in the large flat area towards the Lighthouse, if you search carefully and know what to look for you will find several rare plants, some of them on the British endangered species list. Most of them are minute members of the Pea family. **Fenugreek**, **Knotted Clover**, **Burrowing Clover**, **Slender Bird's-foot Trefoil**, **Bird's-foot** and **Orange Bird's-foot**. Towards the lighthouse large patches of the purple **Viper's Bugloss** live with occasional pink or pure white specimens and across the road nearer the Lighthouse grows another minute plant **Blinks**.

The Lighthouse being built

The Lighthouse was built in 1912 after there had been a number of wrecks on the coast nearby. It now controls the Casquets Light, which was automated in 1992, Point Robert Light in Sark, automated in 1994 and the Channel Light Vessel. The lantern is 109 feet high has an output of 1 million candlepower and a range of 17 miles. It flashes 4 times every 30 seconds. It was electrified in 1976 and the former petrol vapour lamp and clockwork mechanism can be seen in the Museum. On some days you can inspect the lighthouse and climb the tower. Look for the notice on the gate. There is a helicopter landing pad in the grass to the left of the gateway. Until recently when it was automated, the Casquets relief keepers and most of their supplies were flown out from here, replacing two and a half centuries of relief boats from Alderney. The Lighthouse also acts as Alderney's Emergency Station. All 999 calls are routed through here and the appropriate service alerted by the duty keeper.

Take the path on the seaward side of the Lighthouse. As you go down the slope towards the road you pass a patch of **Meadow Rue** growing either side of the path. It usually flowers in August and this is probably the only patch in the wild in the island. In front of you is a pleasant shingle hung bungalow with an interesting wall decoration of fishes made from **Ormer** shells and rows of **Scallop** shells around the concrete plinth. These were all caught locally by the owner some years ago. The house was a former German hut moved to this spot to replace the terrace of eight two-storied 'Back-to-Back' quarry workers houses, built by his grandfather, which the Germans destroyed to clear a field of fire.

Just offshore on a little islet lies Fort Les Hommeaux Florains. It is said that this islet was covered with the wild flowers which gave it its name until the fort was built. It took five years to build and mounted 5 guns. A small drawbridge connected it to the end of a causeway. The 59 men who manned them must have had an uncomfortable time for, as you will see if you pass here at high tide with a sea running, the waves wash right up to the windows.

It was only occupied for about 30 years and was empty when one of Alderney's most famous wrecks occurred here in February 1902. The Sailing Ship *Liverpool* was a 3,400 ton 4-master, with a length of 333ft. 2in. one of the largest sailing-vessels

Wreck of the sailing ship Liverpool, *25th February 1902*

afloat, when in thick fog, with all sails set, she ran gently into the small islet of Les Hommeaux Florains, crowned by its Fort. That morning, John Godfray who lived only a few yards away and had just gone to work in the Quarry near his house saw the ghostly ship with its white masts glide by. Later he and his friend George Sharp heard voices in the fog. They ran for his little boat in the creek in front of his house and pulled quickly out to the ship. They were able to tell the crew who were taking to the boats that they could walk ashore over the island, using the little bridge between two rocks and the shore of Alderney. The crew walked ashore and there was no loss of life.

Liverpool owned by R.W. Leyland, was en route from Antwerp to San Francisco with a cargo of cement, steel girders, marble and foodstuffs, silks, olive oil and wines. Islanders were given permission to help unload the cargo. Her sails were taken down and the yards removed. All of this took some weeks and the great ship sat there on the rocks. Trips were run in *Courier* and other vessels from Guernsey and Weymouth to view the wreck. She eventually broke up and sank. The part of the cargo that did not disappear into the homes of the islanders was sold for £ 10,000. Some of the marble was later used to make a flight of stairs in the Town Hospital in St. Peter Port, where they were in use until the hospital was converted into Police HQ in 1993.

Several other wrecks in the vicinity in a short few years caused Trinity House to build the Lighthouse nearby as a warning to shipping, especially vessels using the Race, whose swift currents merging here with the tidal flow along the French coast can easily push vessels away from their intended course onto the rocks.

A few yards away on the other side of Cat's Bay is Fort Quesnard, called from the name of the point on which it stands (derived from Canard meaning Duck). The barracks part which faces you has its date over the doorway. It accommodated 55 officers and men to serve the battery of 7 guns which was separated from the barracks by a dry moat and drawbridge. There is an interesting association here with one of Britain's most famous soldiers, General Gordon, of Khartoum fame. Whilst serving in Alderney as a young Lieutenant, he was responsible for supervising the construction of this fort.

Note the **Tamarisk** trees along the roadway between the two forts. Many of these will be seen around the island close to the sea, a number of them more than a century old. Your walk continues along the rough track to the left of the road by Fort Quesnard. This was the original road around the island up to

1940. The road now tarmacadamed was put in by the Germans all the way to Longis Bay.

In a small depression flooded in winter just to the left of the two upright poles grows another larger patch of the unusual **Land Quillwort,** described in Walk 5 on Essex Hill. Its leaf-like fronds have usually disappeared by the end of June. Here also in midsummer look for the **Yellow Bartsia**, whose spikes of bright yellow hooded flowers vary from 4in to 2ft in height. This too is a moisture loving plant. It is semi-parasitic on the roots of others. Follow the path in front of the house. All along here in midsummer you will find a variety of butterflies and dragonflies. This is another place to find the **Glanville Fritillary**. Don't confuse it with the similar coloured **Wall** butterfly seen later in the year in August, which has a round black spot on the top wings. **Little Blues** are common, frequently fluttering in pairs. A second brood usually hatches about the middle of August which feast on the nectar from the tiny **Autumn Squills** found all along this track at intervals. Keep an eye open for the **Large White**, **Green-veined White**, the occasional **Red Admiral** and **Small Tortoiseshell** butterflies and very occasionally a bright yellow **Brimstone**.

You next come to Fort Houmet Herbé, meaning 'grassy island'. This elegant fort was built in 1854 and held 61 men to

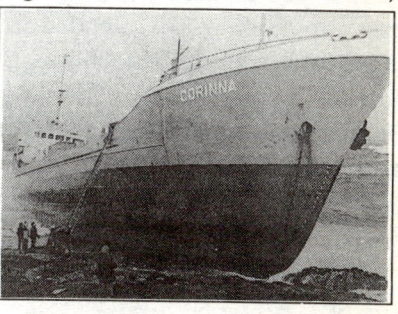

Wreck of MV Corinna, *11th February 1985*

serve its 5 guns. At low tide you can walk across the tidal causeway and look around inside. Offshore is a dangerous, extensive reef, Les Brinchetais or Brimtides. Here barely 10 years ago the MV *Corinna* came to grief.

Corinna was on a regular run between England and the islands with a mixed cargo of furniture, gas cookers, food and liquor. She fell foul of the rapid currents over the Brinchetais Reef and was swept onto the back of Houmet Herbé islet with its ruined Victorian Fort. Perched high and dry at low tide the crew walked to safety and she gave an easy access to the islanders who salvaged a considerable part of her cargo. Much of the liquor was locked up in the old town Jail for security and over the next few weeks various salvage attempts were made, as the vessel was not badly damaged. She defeated all attempts for almost six months, until a particularly high tide and some powerful Dutch tugs combined to release her and she was towed off and repaired.

Fort Houmet Herbé in rough weather

An interesting sequel to the number of new gas cookers that appeared in island homes was that they wouldn't work. Intended for use on town gas, the jets were unsuitable for the bottled gases used in Alderney. One lucky possessor of a box of odd parts, found that he had the entire supply of conversion kits for the cargo of cookers and is reputed to have done very well out of his find, selling the kits to possessors of the useless cookers. This wreck also provided a tourist attraction for months.

This too must have been an uncomfortable posting for the troops. As the photo shows in rough weather the waves wash in through the gateway and reach the musket slits. More of the colourful **Kaffir Fig** grows around the old gun mountings. The rocks to the left of the fort are usually topped on a sunny day, by a line of **Shags** drying their wings. Keep your eyes open too for white birds looking like small Herons on the islet or between here and Longis Bay. These are **Small Egrets**. They have probably come from N. Africa, but at least one has been here through the winters of 1993 and 1994 and during 1994 four were here together for several months. A single **Cattle Egret** joined them for some weeks and might have been seen on many evenings roosting in a tree on the Golf Course near the Nunnery.

In crevices amongst the ridged sandstone rocks just above high water mark, between the fort and the shore, you might find a number of plants growing. Several species of **Rush** and a tiny little plant with pretty pink and white flowers in August, **Sea Milkwort**, a member of the Primrose family. Also here is another of Alderney's specialities, the **Alderney Sea Lavender**, found only here and at a tiny area in Jersey. It too has recently been recognised as a separate species from the other similar Sea Lavenders. Along the edge of the grass look for the creamy-white 4in spikes of **White Stonecrop**. In front of the stone wall here is a large patch of pink **Oxalis**, in flower for many months in the year. It originates in Mexico and can be seen in many grass verges in Alderney. On the wall is a memorial tablet to a Pekinese Dog which died many years ago. In the garden of the house behind the stone wall the rocky outcrop is known as La Petite Folie, another 150yds or so bring you to a much larger outcrop, called appropriately, La Grande Folie.

Between the two is a rocky headland with **Heather** and **Bell-heather** making a bed of colour in August and September. At this time the plants are often smothered with **Silver-Y Moths** feeding on the nectar. Here is another marvellous place to find small plants. In early spring, on a bright sunny day, look for the blue/mauve and white stars of the **Sand Crocus** in the short turf of the well trodden pathways around this headland. At about the same time you may see a few scattered spikes about 3-4in high of the **Green-winged Orchid**. Look over the wall of the large blue-painted cedar house here and you will probably see more of them in the lawn just inside the wall. On the headland too look for **Wild Thyme**, you will often smell it as you walk over it before you see it. Tiny strands of blue and white **Milkwort** flowers appear here in May and June. In August and early September there are masses of **Autumn Squills**, their nectar being supped by large numbers of butterflies, mainly **Common Blue**s.

The next bay along here is Baie de Grounard. The Gurnard is a red fish with a large head often caught about here and makes excellent eating. In the field next to the house, if you approach quietly you will invariably see **Rabbits** grazing up towards the bracken at the top of the field. Look for a large black one, frequently about this spot and perhaps some smaller black rabbits. Alderney has no natural predators except man and the **Kestrel**, often hovering high above you along the track. The black rabbits which are to be seen at several places round the island are thought to be a wild form which, not being well camouflaged like the common form, has survived here because of this lack of natural predators.

There have been several more wrecks around the Brimtides and along this stretch of coast.

Just beyond this little bay close to the beach and along the slight ridge where the grass slopes down to the stones is a botanist's paradise. Here grow several small, even minute, plants, two of them on the endangered species list and only known elsewhere in Britain from the Gower peninsula in Wales. Look amongst the thin turf for **Small Hare's-ear** a tiny member of the parsley family barely an inch high with yellow flowers set in green cups in June. The **Small Rest-harrow**, grows in rosettes about 2-3in across, its pink and white pea flowers appear in May and June, whilst the **Bastard Toadflax** has minute five petalled white flowers on thin olive-green trailing stems from June to October. A few yards further on look for the purple flowers of the stemless or **Ground Thistle** in July to September. The flat rosettes, 4-6in across, of their prickly pale green leaves are easy to spot. In the same area in June and July, see the yellow flowers of the **Carline Thistle** a plant up to a foot high. These dry out and persist throughout the winter. Mauve **Wild Thyme** and white **Eyebright** can be found in flower from May to October.

In July and August the grass here is turned pink and white with the creeping flowering stems of **Rest Harrow**. Unlike the prickly variety more common in England these stems are soft and furry to the touch. Amongst the rocks on the shore in August and September, the very common **Rock Samphire** flourishes. The Grande Folie is now just behind you. Round its base in April and May if you look carefully you may find more of the **Green-winged Orchid**.

Keep along the track skirting the tops of the shingle around several small bays. You reach a more open grassy area with several WD marker stones. At low tide offshore here look for the twin boilers and part of the hull of the SS *Felix de Abasolo* a large Spanish Collier wrecked here in June 1910 in dense fog. No lives were lost.

You have now reached the back of the stone wall built to protect some houses formerly here from stray shots from the firing range. Take the path to the left of the dunes nearest the sea. In late July and early August you might see swarms of large **Emperor Dragonflies** along the bank here, like minute helicopters, newly hatched from Longis Pond a few hundred yards away. Go through the gap above the stones and almost immediately, the grass either side of the track is the unusual **Bermuda Grass**. Flowering in August and September, its 4in. flower stalks carry five red-brown fingers of flowers radiating like the spokes on an umbrella. In May and June in the sand here look for the tiny 2-3in. stems of the **Sand Cat's-tail**, another grass whose name is a perfect description of its appearance.

On your right is the old site of the targets of the Rifle Butts with its safety trench, and in front of you the huge bulk of the German Anti-tank wall which, although never quite completed, runs almost the whole way around the bay. Walk along the beach side to the causeway to Raz Island, the Island of the Race. Also completed in 1855 the fort mounted 10 guns and protected both the bay and its approaches. It was known to the Victorians as 'Rat Island'. It too was sold at auction in 1930. It has been used at various times as a residence, a restaurant and a bird museum. When it was being built a number of stone age and bronze age burials were discovered with tools and weapons of their period in them. Either side of the causeway is a peat bed. From time to time storms have uncovered the stumps of a forest here and in the bay. The peat was laid down originally under freshwater when the high water mark was much further out to sea than at present.

A wooden spear dated to 4,000BC was found here some years back and the shaft of another of about the same age was recovered in 1992. Flint and stone tools going back as much as 150,000 years have also been found.

Look up across the bay to the Hanging Rocks sticking out from the cliff, with below, along the opposite side of the bay the Frying Pan Battery at the left and the row of gun emplacements to its right.

Along the beach you will nearly always find several sorts of **Gull**, the occasional **Curlew** and many **Oyster Catchers**. During the spring and autumn migrations many small waders appear for a week or two. Keep your eyes open for the white forms of the **Egrets** and the frequent **Grey Heron** amongst the rocks as the tide goes down. **Dunlin**, **Stilt**, **Turnstones** and **Plovers** are usually seen at these times.

In the middle of the wall is another gun emplacement with a larger one at the far end. Here the old wall of the Nunnery

Longis Bay, with Essex Castle and the Hanging Rocks

still lies on the beach, several centuries after it collapsed and if the tide has washed the sand away you will see a small part of the old cobbled vraic road just before the last of the German bunkers by the slipway. If you look amongst the stones either side of the Nunnery on the beach you will probably find small pieces of Roman brick or roof tiles.

At low tide the remains of the old jetty, rebuilt in 1660 at a cost of £1,000 tournois (about £ 200 sterling), stick out across the bay. A few years after this was rebuilt the Alderney Court passed a law decreeing a fine for any inhabitant who removed either small or large stones from this jetty. It was virtually abandoned after the "New Pier" was built at Braye in 1736.

This ends your walk. Go up the slipway to the seats. Public toilets can be found in the Portacabin behind you and you can catch the bus by the roadside a few yards off.

6. Inland walks

Walk 12. The Pottery to Pont Martin, La Bonne Terre, Platte Saline and Le Petit Val, returning to the starting point.
(About 1½ -2 miles. Allow 1½ hours)

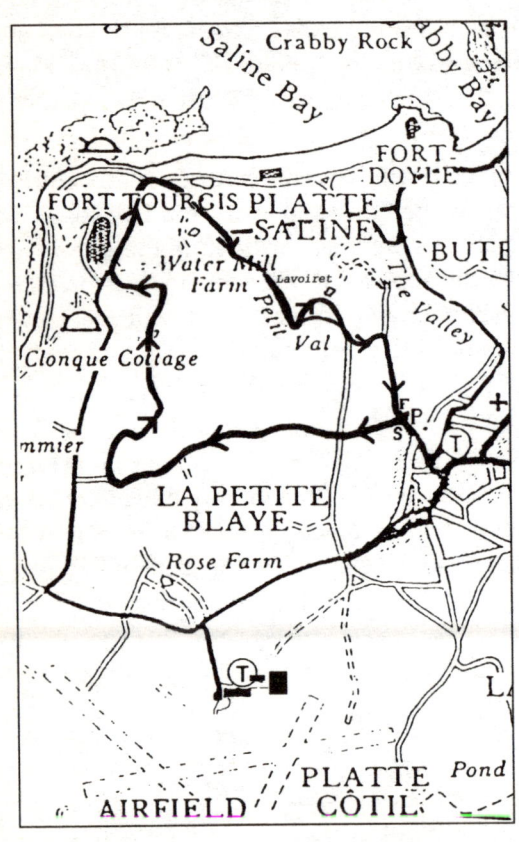

From Royal Connaught Square go up the Mouriaux to the Pottery wall and take the turning to the left, Carrière Viront. Carrièr means 'quarry' but here the word is probably corrupted from charrière, meaning a 'cart track'. Go straight across at the cross roads past the bungalow development of Allée ès Fées, Fairies Lane. This ancient name is an allusion to the possible Neolithic remains on this site around which 'Fairy Rings' of mushrooms often grew.

You cross a field with an excellent view of Fort Tourgis and Platte Saline. This is known as Vue de la Saline and overlooked the salt flats. It forms part of La Petite Blaye open-field system. Follow the track downhill between the bushes. On your left a small wooden gate gives access to the public garden known as St. Vignalis' Garden. He was the monk who reputedly brought Christianity to Alderney about AD 575. The garden contains the old spring fed *abreuvoir publique* or cattle trough, where cattle from this part of the island were brought to drink. The area is beside a natural stone bridge known as Pont Martin from the name of the early 19th century owner of Rose Farm whose land runs to here. This tranquil spot now belongs to the Church and seats and tables are provided where you may picnic.

Behind the trough is a triangular very boggy bank where the islands very few **Spotted** and **Marsh Orchids** grow. The principal stream of the island, originating in fields alongside the airport entrance flows past here and from at least the twelfth century to about 1920 supplied the Watermill at the bottom of the valley. When you leave the garden, turn left and cross the "Bridge". A few yards further on, an ancient apple tree stands at the junction of three paths. Turn right and in about 100yds. cautiously descend the steep bank here. At the bottom you are close to the stream, the path alongside it from the bridge is badly overgrown and was best avoided. This valley is full of **Poplars**, **Sycamores** and **Willows**, it is known as Le Val de la Bonne Terre. The 'good land' referred to is somewhat of a misnomer, it is Bonne pour rien, 'good for nothing'. Many wild flowers will be found along this path and on a warm sunny day it is vibrant with the drone of bees.

Many butterflies will be seen and some of the woodland birds, generally not very frequent in Alderney, look out for **Tree Creepers**. The path winds up and down, never far from the stream bed. As you reach the lower levels it crosses the remains of a wall, far more of which is still to be seen on your right. This was the retaining wall of the mill leat which kept sufficient head of water to drive the machinery. It is now a bog with **Willows** and **Water Mint** in some profusion and many marsh plants including the **Spotted Orchid**. Notice particularly the huge cushions, several feet high and about a yard across, of the **Tussock Sedge**. Rare in the two larger islands, this is absent from Sark and Herm.

Further down duck under a tree and two stepping stones take you across the narrow stream. Here the remains of an old building were possibly a public washplace. The other side of the track housed another cattle trough. This was one of the places where the women came to wash their clothes at the stone lined *Lavoiret*, no longer there. The path widens now between walls and you soon reach another junction. The pump house and filter beds on your right supply a considerable part of the island's fresh water which, as noted in an earlier walk, can now be routed right back to the reservoirs in times of plentiful rain. The tall hedge on your left with hollow stems, heart-shaped leaves and long bunches of tiny white flowers is the **Japanese Knotweed**, a highly invasive plant, member of the Dock family, and often know in the Channel Islands as **"Donkey's Rhubarb"**. Watermill Farm lies just below the trees. The recently reroofed house is probably the oldest in the island, but the mill is completely derelict now.

Take the track up the slope to the left and you reach the road opposite Fort Tourgis. If you haven't already done so, this is a good time to walk in through the gateway, no longer with its drawbridge. Look at the buildings and try to visualise them

Fort Tourgis from Le Petit Val

in their heyday. Under the court yard are huge tanks to store rainwater from the roofs. Another gateway at the opposite end gives access to the outer walls. The building just outside was stabling for the officer's horses. The outer entrance here was made during the war. This space between the walls is filled with the sites of former Victorian gun batteries, several German bunkers and other gateways formerly all with drawbridges to isolate various parts of the fort. You can also gain access to the upper level and enjoy the views from the ramparts.

Return to the roadway and carry on down the hill. This brings you to Platte Saline. Used in olden times as salt pans and for the drying and salting of mackerel and conger eels, a tax of £ 10 a year was paid to the Crown for several centuries for this right of *Éperquerie*. Small boats took quantities of several tons each of dried fish to England annually in the 16th-18th centuries. Until the mid 1960s a large pond here held **Eels** and **Sticklebacks**. Increased water extraction turned it into a bog but heavy winter and spring rains in 1993/4 filled it once again and a **Mallard** raised eight young in the pond before the free water disappeared in the summer of 1994. After about 20 years absence, four clumps of **Galingale**, a sedge known in the Islands as **'Han'** have reappeared here with the increased water level.

The field on your right shows clumps of the large silvery leaves of the **Globe Artichoke**. Their huge flower heads are bright mauve in late July and August. These are self sown from a crop grown in another field about 100yds away in the 1950s and have appeared here in the last three or four years. There are a lot more plants either side of the stream bed a few yards further on. The **Tamarisks** along the wall here were already well grown trees in 1890.

Across the road you are now level with two tall concrete walls. The island's sand pit was just behind these until it became worked out about 1991 and is now gradually being filled in with quarry spoil from the Banquage housing scheme. The walls were built by the Germans with a roadway between them and hoppers above so that the sand could be loaded directly into lorries. There was a small powder magazine just about here in Victorian times.

You have now reached the junction of Route de Picaterre, running parallel with the shore, back towards town and Le Petit Val, which will lead you back to the Pottery.

From this corner the German Slave Camp *Lager Helgoland* stretched along Picaterre for several hundred yards and back up the hill behind. It held about 1,500 slave workers, mostly young Russian men, in wooden sectional huts. The main gate pillars are still there about 100 yards along Picaterre, forming a wide entrance with the large concrete entrance area, in front of a charming bungalow, built, as were many others along this road, about 12-15 years ago. Other buildings and remains of the camp in this area have been converted into garages and outbuildings.

Take the road up the hill. Watermill Farm buildings, newly reroofed are on your right. The hill is quite steep and there is a seat in a small clump of trees half way up in the bend.

Further up, just as you get to a road junction on the right you will note a grassy track leading down on the left at the start of a low stone wall. Growing in the old mortar pointing of the wall about 20ft along is a small patch of **Rusty-back Fern**, the only colony in the island. This will only survive on the lime rich old mortar and cannot grow in cemented walls. Go down the grassy track. At the bottom you will find another of the Victorian *abreuvoirs publiques*. Fed by a small stream running down this valley it was much used in older times.

This area of Alderney is called 'Ladysmith'.

The Lavoiret at Ladysmith

There is some doubt whether it was given this name to celebrate the relief of that town in the South African (Boer) War at the turn of the century, or if it is not a corruption of the old French *Les doüits*. In Guernsey this usually means a man-made ditch with a stream in it, but in Alderney seems to have in the main been used for public washing places. If you look down below the trough about 30ft. you will see the former *lavoiret* where the women of the town did their laundry. If you carry on up the track for about 30 yards there is another leading to the left. Take this down through the trees to the washing place. Somewhat overgrown now, it consists of a low stone

The German Water Tower

Parish Church and Town, NE from German Water Tower

wall with a flat flagstone area inside. In the middle of this, the stream runs in a flat, shallow, stone lined depression. It is protected from development under the Alderney Historic Buildings Law and is cleared and the vegetation cut back occasionally. Its exact date is unknown but it has possibly been here since Elizabethan times. It is the place associated with the legend of the White Bull of Grosse Rock described in Walk 2.

Another 300 yds or so along the road brings you back to the Pottery where, for much of the day, except on a Sunday, you can get some refreshments if you so wish.

Old Church and Town, from German Water Tower

Walk 13. The Inchalla hotel, Val Reuters, Fontaine David, Newtown, Braye Bay, returning to the starting point.
(About 1½ -2 miles, allow 1½ hours).

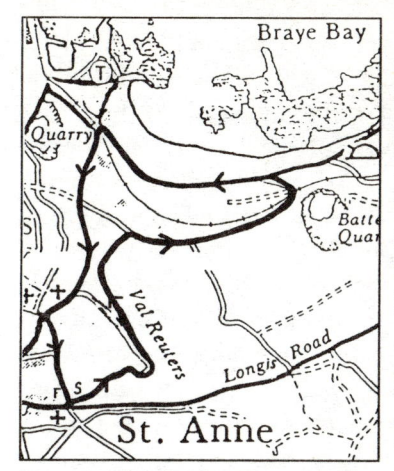

The Inchalla Hotel is at the top of Le Val, on the eastern side of Town. On its right is an alleyway between houses. Take this track, it runs uphill for a few dozen yards and then turns down behind the hotel. It is known as Val Reuters.

The estate of recent houses on the left is known as Auderville, from *Haute de Ville*, 'above the town'. The lane continues between banks and trees and becomes damp. Springs here form into a small stream which feeds a pond in a garden to the left and then continues at the side of the track in an open ditch to an old cattle trough and beyond.

In this part of the valley you may notice the tiny yellow flower heads, followed by a head of red hooked seeds, on 3ft. tall stems of **Herb Bennett**, (sometimes known as **Wood Avens**) and the delicate pale mauve-pink or white flowers of **Enchanter's Nightshade** each with two stamens sticking out, also on stems about 2-3ft. high. As you descend past the cattle trough the hill on your right is Alderney's only **Ash** wood. There are also some very large Ash trees at the bottom of this lane.

Further on, descend a short flight of steps. A recently built garage on the left partially screens the entrance to one of Alderney's German tunnels. This tunnel is about 10ft. high and goes back into the hillside for about half a mile. It was never

Gallery in Water Lane tunnel

fully completed, has four main branches, two of which never reached their intended open ends, with two much taller side galleries, both beautifully cement rendered, along the route. There are the remains of the narrow gauge railway lines in places, several rock falls and a flooded length. On the opposite side of the valley here, set back a short way from the bottom of the steps is the partly blocked entrance to a second similar 5-branched complex. One of the tunnels from this emerges again about 150-200yds further down the lane. For your own safety, do not enter these unless you have a powerful torch, wellington boots and a hard hat and someone else with you.

Carry on down hill on the track. There are a number of interesting trees and shrubs here including a couple of **Wild Plums**. The whole walk is likely to offer you sight and sound of many birds and insects. You are now in the part known as Fontaine David, collectively the whole route is known to locals as "the Water Lanes". On the left down this part two other tracks allow you to slip through into the upper lane if you wish to shorten your route and regain Braye Road not far from the Catholic church, built since the war to replace the former one at Crabby. If you continue on, you reach a part, sometimes known as Bailiff's Lane from the family who owned the property here last century. About here a long flight of steps behind some houses also leads back to Braye Road. In Victorian times another lane ran down here, parallel to Braye Road, and with a stream in it. This was put into a brick culvert about the turn of the century. It was known as Bottle Alley and the lower end can still be traced as a green lane about 20ft. wide between more recent houses. It used to emerge exactly opposite the present gates of the school in Newtown Road. If you look over the wall to the left of the bungalow opposite the gates when you reach this spot, you will see the lane, bounded by garden walls.

Follow the road as it turns right. In early spring you may see the white flower heads on 12-18in. stalks of the **Hairy Onion**, similar in appearance to and a very close relative of, the slightly more elegant **Star of Bethlehem**. As you near the bottom. on the right is one of the old covered well heads and, immediately beyond, the former building which housed the gas works. The curved wall of the Harbour Lights bar is a few yards further still. You can obtain refreshments or a bar lunch here in comfort. There is also a sheltered outdoor patio for warm weather eating. The wooden building opposite the end of the lane is the water pumping station.

Newtown and Gasworks about 1920

If you turn right here, follow Newtown Road until you come to the Battery Quarry on your right. Cross the railway lines and follow the Lower Road back to Braye Station. You can make your way back to Town from here by any of several routes, the most direct being straight up the main road following the sign pointing to "La Ville". Most of the points of interest along this part have already been covered in previous walks.

Alternatively, turn left and pass the school, to reach Braye Road sooner.

Walk 14. The Inchalla Hotel, via Longis Road to Valongis, descending to Newtown, and returning via the footpath to Les Rochers.

(About 2 miles, allow 1-1½ hours).

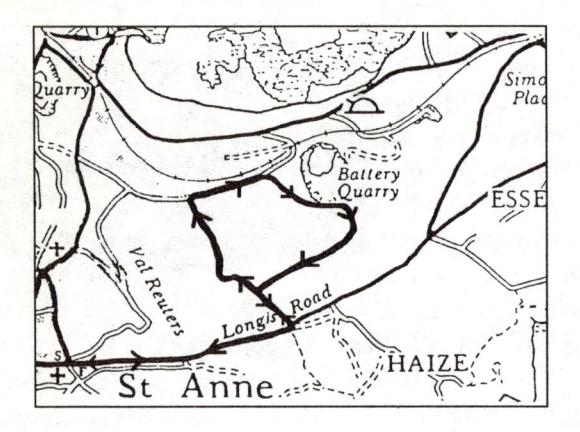

From the Inchalla go to the junction of High Street and Le Val and turn left into Longis Road. The Telephone Exchange is a few yards along on your left. Past the line of newer bungalows is a stone house against the road. This was at one time a public house, was derelict for many years and has recently been converted into an attractive private house. A little further on is Verdun Farm lying a bit back from the road. The fields are behind but it is no longer a working farm. They have an interesting flora with **Black Mullein** and **Star of Bethlehem** growing in some of them and another of the island's trig points. The large white house behind a tall stone wall is "The Vines" until his death in 1992, the home for many years of well known cricket commentator John Arlott. A plaque on the wall recalls this. Originally called "Balmoral" it was built in the early part of the century and run as a hotel between the wars. After the last war it became Les Becquets Hotel for some years.

The next turning on the left is Champs Beulai, a recent housing estate. The name appears as Champs Reullez in a charter of 1572, from the Old French *rouillés* meaning unused land. 'Champs' in the Bailiwick is usually used to describe a field not enclosed by a hedge.

A little further on, Valongis is on the same side of the road. On its corner is the Cimitière St Michel, the 'Stranger's Cemetery', the origins of which have already been described. Turn into Valongis. At the junction with the gravel track on the right the field is part of the Church Glebe land. It too has some interesting plants, probably the result of cultivation in days gone by. Carry on down the hill which twists and turns. Either side are banks of **Hart's-tongue Fern** under the trees. The fields of Verdun Farm run down to the road here and on the next corner is a ruined building. Behind this is a vertical drop into a small quarry. Keep on the road and past the house the track leading into the quarry is on your left. Several moisture loving plants thrive in the damp soil caused by the spring here including more **Hart's-tongue Fern**. The valley is for the most part filled with self-sown **Sycamore** trees, probably the most successful tree in the island. On the right down a drop behind some Victorian railings is another of the *abreuvoirs publiques* or cattle troughs fed from the spring in the quarry. The paved track leading to it might also have been one of the washing places in former times. Another ruined dwelling lies on your left at the next junction.

Turn right and in about 200yds take the grassy track just before the plantation of conifers. Above you is the huge dish of the TV relay and above that the tall mast of the other TV and radio aerials. The path winds up the hillside past the mast and comes onto the level top of Les Rochers, called from the two sets of standing stones here, probably another Neolithic burial site. Along the track are several more German bunkers and gun emplacements. mostly now hidden in vegetation. In midsummer you will find the quite large mauve/blue flowers of **Meadow Cranesbill** along here, one of its few sites in Alderney, an occasional pink specimen might be noticed. In August and September look for more **Wild Clematis** in flower here near the bunkers.

Deep in the hill below you are more partially built German tunnels connecting to the complex of bunkers along the Longis Road. The open space on the right is more or less surrounded by the stones of Le Grand Rocher and the old stone building just beyond, newly converted into a house was one of two powder magazines built here in the early 18th century for the militia. A large square fort and barracks was projected nearby, to overlook Braye Bay, but was never constructed.

A few more yards brings you back to the Church Glebe and you can return to Town the way you came.

Interior of "The Rink" cinema, after the Germans turned it into a luxury theatre in 1942

Walk 15. Val Fontaine to La Haize, Essex Castle, the Devereux house Hotel and Barrack Master's Lane, returning via Bluestone Hill
(About 1½ -2 miles, allow 1½ hours)

The starting point for this walk is in Longis Road by the two houses on the right before the junction by the Golf Club.

Take the short turning to the left of these two houses. This leads downhill to another *abreuvoir publique* known since before the 16th century as La Blanche Fontaine. Close by is a well and a pump house. Just beyond in the trees are the ruins of a building. This is described in a charter of Elizabeth I as "the house known as the White Fountain, formerly a public washing place". The line of the road possibly follows the line of an old Roman road leading from Longis Bay up to the fertile agricultural land on the Blayes. In Victorian times parts of it were cobbled and at the far end, at the bay, the former vraic road was a continuation of the track.

Follow the road to the first track and turn uphill. The building immediately on your left is the Devereux House Hotel, previously the Essex House Hotel. (Both names commemorate the association of Queen Elizabeth's Earl of Essex who held the "Fee-farm" or tenancy of Alderney from the Crown from about 1590 until he was beheaded in 1601. It is unlikely that he ever visited the island however). Before the hotel, a building on this site was the Barrack Master's House in the 1850s and earlier still the home farm of the Governors of Alderney who owned Essex Hill and Castle.

The White Fountain

The small stone house on the left up this track was also once a public house. More recently it was run as a bar annex to the hotel but has been a private house for some years. The original bar counter forms the divide between the kitchen and living room and this room goes the full height of the house and has a gallery round it. Behind this again, approached from either the track or the house is a well house. The deep well in Victorian times held a pump to supply Fort Essex. The spring feeding the well overflows further down the lane past the hotel and runs thence to the sea at the Nunnery.

Carry on up the track until it divides. Take the left hand branch and you are soon at the top of Essex Hill by the large German Anti-aircraft Battery and the Trig. point. Follow the road down round the outside of the Fort to the bottom of the hill by the Essex Manor Restaurant and take the grassy track to the left just past the stone pillars. This is the bottom of Barrack Master's Lane.

In a few yards make your way to the left up the narrow track between the trees. This brings you into the bottom of the quarry which gave this part of Longis Road, now about 75 yards behind you, the name of Bluestone Hill.

Here is the almost circular entrance to another German Tunnel. This one was completed. It runs in a semicircle, emerging about 200 yards further up Barrack Master's Lane and also has two high smooth rendered galleries inside and the remains of some of the railway track. You can safely go into it for about 25 yards, but as it turns and becomes dark return to the entrance. It is flooded and not safe to go further. Continue up the lane. The stream in the valley bottom here is the only one in the island which connects directly with the sea. Before the war eels were caught here, but none have been reported for many years.

The island sewer from Town runs underground alongside, to the filter beds at the Nunnery. You will notice several ferns under the trees, **Hart's-tonque**, **Male Fern** and **Lady Fern** are the most common. **Elderberry** bushes are frequent and there are some well grown trees. This sheltered valley is another favourite spot for birds and butterflies and you will probably see the primitive spikes of the **Common Horsetail** alongside the track in the damper spots. As you reach the more open part before the hotel, on the left along the edge of the trees on the bank above you are tall plants often 6ft or more high of the **Globe Artichoke**, their huge mauve flowers prominent in August. In the wall nearby you will hear the tinkling sound of the stream coming from the well you passed earlier.

Robert Devereux, 2nd Earl of Essex

Opposite the hotel just before you reach the tarmac road again a track on the right will also take you back to the main road. On its corner the very tall grass (3-5ft.) in flower for much of the summer has the peculiar name of the **Rescue Brome**. On your right before it, the pink flowered plants with rounded soft leaves are another colony of the **Alderney Geranium**. Follow either back to your starting point.

This ends the last of these fifteen walks round Alderney.

ALDERNEY BY CAR

For the benefit of those whose time here is short, or who cannot tackle all the walks, if you have hired a car, this chapter will offer you a 'Round the Island Trip' taking in some parts of the island not covered on the tour bus routes.

For more detailed information about the places you pass en route, refer to the page in this guide noted at various points along your route.

Gate pillars of Lager Borkhum

For a map of this route, follow the larger map, the frontispiece of the book. Start at the top of High Street, at the junction with Le Val, and take the Longis Road. In about a quarter of a mile, the large white house on the left seen between the gate pillars of a high stone wall is 'The Vines'. Note the Heritage Plaque on its wall recalling its occupation by John Arlott. (Walk 14, p. 128) You next pass Champs Beulai, a turning on the left, followed by Valongis (p. 129). On the corner of this road is the 'Stranger's Cemetery' (Walk 4, p. 55). The Catholic Cemetery, is next, its entrance just past the next house on the left (p. 53). The turning opposite leads to the *Impôt*, the island's rubbish dump, passing between two sets of pillars marking the entrances to the German Camp *Lager Borkhum* (Walk 4, p. 53). As you descend the hill past some open fields, the Golf Clubhouse is on your right with Alderney's bowling green in front of it on the left. At the bottom of the hill, the road leading up to Fort Essex (Walk 5, p. 60), is on the right. Take this to the end of the tarmac, from where you can enjoy the views of the French coast, with Jersey down on the horizon and extensive views of Longis Bay and across the island to the harbour and Fort Albert as you return to the bottom. The 'Odeon' or German Fire Control Tower (Walk 11, p. 106) dominates the skyline to its right. The Essex Manor Restaurant is on your right as you pass the two stone pillars at the bottom of this hill. Turn right at the main road and in about 100yds. right again into the car park behind the Nunnery. (Walk 5, p. 62). Here are public toilets and seats to admire the view in front of you.

Across the bay, Fort Ile de Raz (Island of the Race), known to the Victorians as Rat Island (Walk 11, p. 116) sits on its islet, joined to Alderney by the long causeway, which is always covered at high spring tides. On your left the huge semicircular sweep of the German anti-tank wall now forms an ideal protection for sunbathers and picnicers. On your right below half-tide you can see the remains of the 1660 jetty of the Longis Harbour, (Walk 11, p. 117).

Returning to the main road, again turn right and follow the line of the coast across Longis Common. As you leave the car park the row of red brick houses 200 yards up the turning in front of you is 'Coastguards'

Bungalow on Longis Common built from the Commandant's House

Built in 1905 to house the men manning the Coastguard Station on top of Essex Hill. The house on the common nearer you is called 'The Kennels' a name whose origins seem to be forgotten. The reed bed surrounding Longis Pond is on your left and the targets of the old firing range close to the sea on your right. At the side of the road in the left hand verge you might notice a square stone with 450 carved into its top. This is one of a series marking the distance to the targets for the riflemen to set their sights.

On the left, the first house is a large shingle hung bungalow. The central part of this was built for the Commandant of Sylt Concentration Camp and was originally sited at Val L'Emauve, above the south cliffs. It was moved here after the war and the two wings added. A smaller German hut is next door. The remaining houses here were built by the British Ministry of Works after the war to replace some demolished by the Germans.

The road continues up a rise, at the top a driveway leads down to another 'Ministry house'. There are excellent views of the French coast all the way along here on a clear day, and around 1.30-2pm every day you will see the car ferry from

Mannez Pond and the Engine Shed

Guernsey making its way to Weymouth and a Commodore Shipping cargo ferry taking freight the other way.

On the left a rough track leads up to the 'Odeon'. You can follow this carefully and enjoy the panoramic view all round the island from the top by the tower. Below you to the NE is Mannez Quarry, with the end of the railway line and a newly built shed to house the engines. Behind this is the open water of Mannez Pond (Walk 11, p. 107) and to its left a clear view of the Lighthouse. From the other side of the tower, Fort Corblets lies to the west, with Berry's Quarry and, in the distance, Fort Albert with the Town further round to the south. With your back to the tower, the whole of the central part of Alderney, the golf course and Essex Hill is before you and as you complete the circle, Longis Bay and the Forts along the east coast.

Return to the main road, turn left and take the next turning on the right. In a few yards a rocky outcrop frames a view of Fort Houmet Herbé (p. 111). The flag pole in the garden of the house on your left is actually a spar from the wreck of the *Liverpool*. As you pass another 'Ministry house' on your right Fort Quesnard lies in front of you with Fort Les Hommeaux Florains just offshore (pp. 109-10). Past these forts on the corner observe the Ormer and Scallop shell decorations on the walls of another former German hut, moved here to replace more destroyed houses. The Lighthouse is just beyond.

The road now runs along the N. side of the island. Take the turning on the right by the entrance to Fort Corblets (Walk 11, p. 104). Another car park here offers the chance to sit and watch the waves. This is an excellent swimming beach and has good surf when the wind is coming from the northern quarters. Beyond the left hand end of the beach is Arch Bay with Château à L'Etoc beyond. The original telegraph cable to England entered the water just here when it was laid in the 1860s.

Saye Bay is next on your right, with the Camp Site behind its dunes. Here are more toilets, a telephone and, in the season when the camp is occupied, a shop. This was the site during the war of *Lager Norderney* another slave camp holding about 1,500, prisoners, mainly, French, Spanish, Poles, Algerians and Jews. (Walk 10, p. 101). Beyond Saye Farm you can take the track out to Bibette Head. Here a colossal system of fortifications, gun emplacements and an infantry strongpoint were established during the war to cover the entrance to the harbour. Extending right up the hill to the walls of Fort Albert is a series of bunkers, some of them interconnected. The mound out to the point is surrounded with gun emplacements and surmounted by various shelters and mortar points. On the tip of the point the huge bunker was well camouflaged by small rocks cemented all over it.

Return to the road and turn right again. At the top of the rise on your left stop and study the Hammond Memorial (p. 101). Towards Longis Bay, this overlooks the area on the common where more than 300 of the slave workers were buried.

The collection of States' houses known as Whitegates is next, built as married quarters for the Victorian garrisons. Just beyond these, another rough track takes you up to Fort Albert with magnificent views of the Harbour, Braye and Town. (Walk 10, p. 98). From here as you return The Arsenal and Mount Hale are below you on the right (Walk 9, p. 96). At the bottom of the track is the pavilion and pitch of the Alderney Football Club. Once again turn right and follow the road along Braye Bay. On the rocks in the middle, if the tide is low look out for the three wrecks, (Walk 9, p. 91). On reaching Braye Road Station of the Alderney Railway Society, you encounter a one-way system. Go straight over the level crossing and turn right at the end. This takes you back to the harbour. Little Crabby Harbour (the 'New Harbour'), the Braye Chippy, Harbour

House and the Sailing Club are on your left. The Commercial Quay is in front of you. If it is not a boat day you can drive out to the end of the quay and study the yachts and ships in the harbour. An excellent view of Fort Grosnez and the Breakwater can be had from here. Return past the R.N.L.I. Station to the 'Old Harbour' and Braye Street. (Walk 8, p. 87). After crossing the rail tracks. immediately turn right again and at the T-junction turn left. The Old Stables with the exhibition of artefacts from the Elizabethan Wreck is in front of you. If the door is open, stop and go in. (p. 82).

Outside on the left is the island's Power station and York Hill Quarry. Crabby Bay is on the right. At the far end of the bay, Fort Doyle is on the headland and the Ambulance Station on the left of the road. The turning just beyond it takes you up to the Mignot Memorial Hospital. A little further on the right is the slip road down onto Platte Saline. If you take this, travel gently, the sandy track below is firm but uneven. You may follow this past the houses, bungalows and tennis courts to Fort Platte Saline. Now used as a store by the principal builder's merchants. The road runs along the edge of the beach and rejoins the tarmac below Fort Tourgis (Walk 6, p. 74). Take the narrow road by the sea to the car park. From here you have a superb view of the Swinge with, from right to left in front of you, the Grosse Rock, the Nannels Reef, Burhou and Little Burhou, Ortac, the Casquets, Fort Clonque and Les Gardiens rocks, with Guernsey often visible in the distance. (See Walk 2).

Return to the main road and go up Tourgis Hill. You might like to stop by the entrance to the fort and have a brief look inside. Almost at the top of the hill is the small Neolithic Dolmen known as the Roc à

Trois Vaux Valley and Les Gardiens

l'Epine, (Rock in the Thorns). The capstone of this is aligned E-W and at the spring and autumn solstice the sun sets in line with it. From here you get an excellent view of the swift tides in the Swinge, or at slack water will often see yachts and small craft making their way to Braye Harbour from Guernsey. The white navigation cone is nearby to help shipping through the Swinge.

In about half a mile the main road turns left towards the airport. Go straight on and at the next junction follow the rough track out to 'The Guns' (Walk 2 also gives details of most of what you will see for the next mile or so). After viewing the Gannet colony on Les Gardiens, return to the tarmac road and turn right. Almost immediately the tarmac surface ends. You are at the head of Trois Vaux with the stream and a cattle trough nearby. This is the old military road and will take you right round the outside of the airport. Here you pass much closer to the Telegraph Tower. On the left just beyond it, another track runs between two square pillars. These are the entrance to *Lager Sylt*, the only Concentration Camp built on British soil during the Second World War. You can still trace the concrete bases of the huts around the site and note the peculiar concrete sentry boxes, shaped like a bullet, one now at the side of the airport and the other across the old military road on the slight rise opposite. The inmates here wore the blue and white striped 'pyjamas' of the European camps. It was set up at first as a camp for the OT (Organisation Todt) labourers, but after a few months became the headquarters of an SS work battalion. Many of the

Fire-proof Sentry box at Sylt Camp

prisoners here were disaffected Germans, including a number of high ranking Wehrmacht officers who disagreed with Hitler's policies. It was disbanded, burnt and the SS guards and their prisoners returned to Germany, shortly after D-Day in 1944. Some escaped on the way and the survivors were eventually liberated by the Americans in 1945.

The road now undulates across a number of small watered valleys. Most have an old *abreuvoir publique* below the road, some with a cobbled area around. As you go down the first dip, (Val L'Emauve) on your left in the bracken look out for the former site of the Commandant's bungalow, with a tunnel leading into the camp in the hillside behind it. At the 'Madonna Stone' the roadway turns left and passes the end of the airport runway. When you once again reach the tarmac road turn right, and right again in a few hundred yards. You are now in the Chemin du Meunier, the Miller's Road and at the T-junction turn left and you are back at your starting point.

This brings your tours of Alderney, on foot, on a bicycle, or by car to an end. During them you will have seen most of the island, a fair proportion of its fortifications from the Elizabethan period to the Second World War, and some of its wildlife.

You may not have been lucky enough to encounter in the daytime another Alderney speciality, the **Blonde Hedgehog**. The island has a race of these shy nocturnal animals which have blonde quills and the normal brown eyes and feet. These are present in almost equal numbers to the more usual brown variety. It has long been rumoured that Alderney's Hedgehogs had no fleas because the first pair were brought to the island after the war, bought from Harrod's in London. Like **Frogs** and **Toads**, the animal is certainly not native to the island and it is probable that none of these were found here before the war, but, because of the lack of predators they have prospered since and the hedgehog at least is now present in considerable

Corblets and Arch beaches on a busy day in midsummer

numbers. A survey was carried out in 1993 of over 100 animals, many of which were equipped temporarily with miniature radio transmitters so that their movements could be tracked. None of them were found to be infested with fleas, a very definite difference from most UK specimens.

The Alderney Tourist Committee, the Chamber of Commerce, the hoteliers, guest house proprietors, the people of the island and especially the author, hope that you have enjoyed your visit to our quiet and peaceful home and will return another year.

Brian Bonnard
December 1994

INDEX

A
Abreuvoir publique, 123, 131, 141
Albert Gate, 9
Albert House Inn, 28
Alderney Court, 3
Alderney Cricket Club, 30
Alderney Fire Station, 18
Alderney Football Club, 138
Alderney Geranium, 94, 133
Alderney Journal, 2
Alderney Lighthouse, 108
Alderney Pottery, 118, 124
Alderney Railway Society, 83, 88, 138
Alderney Sailing Club, 85
Alderney Sea Lavender, 113
Alderney Society Museum, 15
Alderney Week, 71
Ambulance Station, 82, 139
Arch Bay, 103, 137
Arsenal, The, 90, 98, 138
Ash Wood, 125
Auderville, 125

B
Bacchanalia, 70
Battery Quarry, 93, 127
Beaumont-Hague, 6
Belle Vue Hotel, 29, 80
Berry's Quarry, 137
Bibette Head, 100, 138
Blanche Fontaine, La, 131
Blue Bridge, 71
Bluestone Beach, 51
Bourgage, Le, 22
Brandons, Les, 70
Braye Common, 90
Braye Road Station, 138
Breakwater, 84, 139
Brinchetais Reef, 112
Bronze Age settlement, 63
Burhou, 36, 74, 139
Butes, 30, 80

C
Cachalière Pier, 48
Camp Site, 100, 138
Campania Inn, 27
Cap de la Hague, 6
Casquets, 35, 139
Casquets, legend of, 35
Casquets, wrecks on, 34
Casquets Lighthouse, 34
Cat's Bay, 110
Cathedral of the Channel Islands, 1
Catholic Cemetery, 134
Catholic church, 29, 97, 126
Chaise à la Moine, 72
Château à L'Etoc, 101, 103, 137
Chez André Hotel, 28
Children's Playground, 89
Cimitière St. Michel, 55, 129
Coastguard Lookout point, 57
Coastguard Station, 135
Commercial Quay, 85
Corblets Bay, 104
Corblets Quarry, 94, 104
Corinna, MV, 112
Coronation Inn, 27
Costière, 47
Courier, SS, 110
Court of Heritage, 12
Courthouse, 13
Crabby Bay, 81, 139

D
Dartford Warbler, 48
Devereux House Country Hotel, 131
Devil's Chair, legend of, 72

INDEX

Diver's Inn, 87
Douglas Quay, 87
Doüit, 36

E
Earl of Essex, 131
Elizabethan Wreck, 82, 104, 139
Éperquerie, 121
Essex Castle, 60, 131
Essex Hill, 57, 102, 131
Essex Manor Restaurant, 61, 132, 135
Evacuation commemorative plaque, 85

F
Fontaine David, 126
Fort Albert, 93, 98, 99, 137
Fort Clonque, 37, 68, 78, 139
Fort Corblets, 104, 137
Fort Doyle, 81, 139
Fort Essex, 60, 132, 134
Fort Grosnez, 83, 139
Fort Houmet Herbé, 111, 137
Fort Les Hommeaux Florains, 109, 137
Fort Quesnard, 110, 137
Fort Raz, 60, 135
Fort Tourgis, 73, 120, 139

G
Gannet Colony, 33, 140
Garden Rocks, 33, 139
Georgian House, 28
German Slave Camps, 53, 122
German Tunnels, 125, 130, 132
Giffoine, 32
Glanville Fritillary, 68
Gluie torches, 70
Godfray, John, 109

Golf Club, 131, 134
Government House, 14
Grand Hotel, 31, 81
Grosse Rock, 78, 139
Guernsey 'Donkeys', 59

H
Hammond Memorial, 101, 138
Hanging Rocks, 52
Hanging Rocks, legends of, 59
Hannaine Bay, 78
Hereditary Governors, 9
Houmet Herbé, 112

I
Impôt, 56
Inchalla Hotel, 125
Iron Age Site, 63
Island flag, 13
Island Hall, 14

J
Jubilee Home, 21

L
La Hêche, 46
La Tchue, 51
Ladysmith, 123
Lady Borkhum, 53, 134,
Lager Norderney, 138
Lager Sylt, 136, 140
Landmark Trust, 69
Lavoiret, 36
Lavoiret at Bonne Terre, 120
Lavoiret at Ladysmith, 123
Les Brandons, old custom, 70
Les Hommeaux Florains, 109
Les Huguettes, 63
Les Porciaux, 64

Les Rochers, 128, 129
Leyland, R. W., 110
Lion Rock, 105
Liverpool,
  Sailing Ship, 109, 110, 137
Longis Bay, 135
Longis Beach, 65
Longis Common, 63, 101
Longis jetty, 61, 117, 135
Longis Pond, 135
Lover's Chair, legends of, 41

M
Madame Robilliard's Nose, 59
Madonna Stone, 44, 46, 141
Mannez Pond, 107, 137
Mannez Quarry, 83, 105, 137
Marais Hall Hotel, 19
Marais Square, 18
Masonic Hall, 14
Methodist Chapel, 29, 80
Mignot Memorial
  Hospital, 81, 139
Mill leat, 120
Minerva Camp, 54
Monk's Chair, legend of, 72
Mount Hale Battery, 93, 138
Mouriaux House, 14
Museum, 15

N
Navigation cone, Tourgis, 140
New Harbour, 83, 138
Newtown, 92, 127
Nunnery, The, 56, 62, 135

O
Odeon, The, 106, 135
Old Harbour, 85, 87, 139
Old Parish Church, 25

Ortac, 36, 139
Ortac, legend of, 36
Oven, The, 36

P
Parish church, 9
Peacehaven, 88
Petite Blaye, La, 78
Platte Saline, 36, 67, 81, 139
Platte Saline Battery, 82
Police Station, 13
Pont Martin, 118, 119
Princess Alexandra visit, 17
Princess Elizabeth visit, 16
Public School, 24, 95
Puffins, 68

Q
Quatre Vents, 47
Queen's visit 1957, 24
Queen's visit 1989, 30
Queen Victoria's visit, 25

R
R.N.L.I. Station, 87, 139
Race, The, 110
Raised beach, 69
Raz Island, 60
Riduna Bus Service, 7
Roc à l'Epine, 140
Roman Fort, 62
Rose and Crown, 23
Roselle Point, 99
Round the Island Trip, 134
Route de Suffrance, 48
Royal Alderney Junior Militia, 102

S
Sailing Club, 139
Salvation Army Citadel, 23

Saye Bay, 100, 138
Scottish Presbyterian Church, 21
Sharp, George, 109
Sorcier, 59
St. Anne's Club, 97
St. Martins, 17
St. Vignalis' Garden, 119
States' Chamber, 13
States of Alderney, The, 2
Stranger's Cemetery, 55, 129, 134
Sugar-loaf navigation cone, 51
Swinge, The, 99, 139
Sylt Concentration camp, 140

T
Telegraph Bay, 38
Telegraph Tower, 39, 40
Telephone Exchange, 128
Town, 1, 9
Trois Vaux, 37

V
Val de la Bonne Terre, 119
Val des Portes, 96

Val du Saou, 47
Val L'Emauve, 41, 136, 141
Val Reuters, 125
Vau Pommier, 71
Vau Trembliers, 105
Verdun Farm, 128
Vraic Roads, 62, 71, 92

W
War memorial, 28
Water Lanes, 126
Watermill Farm, 120
White Bull of Grosse Rock, legend of, 36
Whitegates, 92, 98, 138
Windmill, 49
Wrecks in Braye Bay, 91

Y
York Hill Quarry, 82, 139
Youth Club, 30

Z
Zig-Zag, The, 68, 77

The author wishes to express his thanks to the following for permission to use ten of the illustrations used in this work.

Colour photos are by the author, except;

Aerial view of the Island by kind permission of Richard's Newsagents; Gannets by the late Rev. Trevor Collins; Puffin, Dartford Warbler, Blond Hedgehog and Black Rabbit from paintings by Wendy Bramall for the Alderney 1994 Stamp issue, by kind permission of the Guernsey Post Office.

Halftone illustrations are by the author, or from his collection of old photographs, except; Grand Hotel aerial view by Gp. Capt E.F. Odoire; Grand Hotel on fire by Graham Lawson; German Naval funeral from the collection of the Alderney Society Museum; MV *Armas* from the collection of the late Jack Quinain.

NOTES

NOTES

NOTES

NOTES

NOTES

NOTES